2019 SQA Specimen and Past Papers with Answers

Higher

MODERN STUDIES

2018 & 2019 Exams
and 2018 Specimen Question Paper

SQA Higher MODERN STUDIES

This book contains the official SQA 2018 and 2019 Exams, and the 2018 Specimen Question Paper for Higher Modern Studies, with associated SQA-approved answers modified from the official marking instructions that accompany the paper.

In addition the book contains study skills advice. This advice has been specially commissioned by Hodder Gibson, and has been written by experienced senior teachers and examiners in line with the Higher syllabus and assessment outlines. This is not SQA material but has been devised to provide further guidance for Higher examinations.

Hodder Gibson is grateful to the copyright holders, as credited on the final page of the Answer section, for permission to use their material. Every effort has been made to trace the copyright holders and to obtain their permission for the use of copyright material. Hodder Gibson will be happy to receive information allowing us to rectify any error or omission in future editions.

Hachette UK's policy is to use papers that are natural, renewable and recyclable products and made from wood grown in well-managed forests and other controlled sources. The logging and manufacturing processes are expected to conform to the environmental regulations of the country of origin.

Orders: please contact Bookpoint Ltd, 130 Park Drive, Milton Park, Abingdon, Oxon OX14 4SE. Telephone: (44) 01235 827827. Fax: (44) 01235 400454. Email education@bookpoint.co.uk Lines are open 9.00–5.00, Monday to Friday, with a 24-hour message answering service. Visit our website at www.hoddereducation.co.uk. If you have queries or questions that aren't about an order, you can contact us at hoddergibson@hodder.co.uk

This collection first published in 2019 by
Hodder Gibson, an imprint of Hodder Education,
An Hachette UK Company
211 St Vincent Street
Glasgow G2 5QY

Typeset by Aptara, Inc.

Printed in the UK

A catalogue record for this title is available from the British Library

ISBN: 978-1-5104-7829-9

2 1

2020 2019

Introduction

Higher Modern Studies

This book of SQA past papers contains the question papers used in the 2018 and 2019 exams (with the answers at the back of the book). A specimen question paper reflecting the requirements, content and duration of the revised exam in 2019 is also included. All of the question papers included in the book provide excellent, representative practice for the final exams.

Using the past papers as part of your revision will help you to develop the vital skills and techniques needed for the exam, and will help you to identify any knowledge gaps you may have.

It is always a very good idea to refer to SQA's website for the most up-to-date course specification documents. Further details can be found in the Higher Modern Studies section on the SQA website: https://www.sqa.org.uk/sqa/47924.html

The course

You will have studied the following three units:

- Democracy in Scotland and the United Kingdom
- Social Issues in the United Kingdom
- International Issues

Your teacher will usually have chosen one topic from each of the three sections above and you will answer questions on these in your exam (see table below).

Unit of the course	**Option one**	**Option two**
Democracy in Scotland and the UK	Democracy in Scotland	Democracy in the UK
Social Issues in the UK	Social Inequality	Crime and the Law
International Issues	World Powers	World Issues

The exam

This consists of two exam papers and an assignment all externally marked:

- Higher question papers
  80 marks allocated – 73% of the overall marks
- Higher assignment
  30 marks allocated – 27% of the overall marks

Total marks available = 110

The marks you achieve in the question papers and assignment are added together and an overall grade will be awarded. The grade is based on your total marks. Based on notional difficulty, 77 and above (70% and above) is an A; 66–76 (60%–69%) is a B; and 55–65 (50% to 59%) is a C.

The question papers

Question paper 1

You will have 1 hour and 45 minutes to complete this question paper with a total of 52 marks allocated. There are three sections with each section worth between 12 and 20 marks. Overall you will answer two 20 marks and one 12 marks extended response questions.

You will answer **one** question from each section. In the Democracy section, you will have a choice of three questions. In the Social Issues and World Issues sections, you will answer one question from a choice of two from your chosen study.

Question paper 2

You will have 1 hour and 15 minutes to complete three mandatory skills-based questions with a total of 28 marks allocated. Questions 1 and 2 are both allocated 10 marks with question 3 worth 8 marks.

In the exam papers, more marks are awarded for knowledge and understanding than skills so it is crucial that you have a sound grasp of content.

Skills or source-based questions

The three types of skills questions that you will answer are as follows:

Question 1

You will assess the skill of **detecting and explaining the degree of objectivity**. You will be presented with between two and four sources of information which may be in a written, numerical or pictorial form.

"**To what extent is it accurate to state that...**"

Question 2

You will assess the skill of **drawing and supporting conclusions**. You will be presented with between two and four sources of information which may be in a written, numerical or pictorial form.

"**What conclusions can be drawn...**"

Question 3

You will assess the skill of **evaluating the reliability of sources**. You will be presented with between two and four sources of information which may be in a written, numerical or pictorial form.

"**To what extent are Sources A, B and C reliable? You must provide an overall conclusion on the most reliable source.**"

As preparation for your exam, the best advice would be to practise source-based questions and to review the types of information required by an examiner for full marks. Remember, all the answers in source-based questions are contained within the sources. No marks are awarded for additional knowledge.

Knowledge (or extended response) questions

In the knowledge section of your exam you could be asked questions that have a similar style to the following:

- **Discuss – 20-mark extended response**, for example:

  The political system provides an effective check on the government.

  Discuss with reference to a world power you have studied.

- **To what extent – 20-mark extended response**, for example:

  To what extent has a world issue you have studied had an impact in different countries?

- **Evaluate – 12-mark extended response**, for example:

  Evaluate the effectiveness of an electoral system you have studied in providing fair representation.

  You should refer to electoral systems used in Scotland or the United Kingdom or both in your answer.

- **Analyse – 12-mark extended response**, for example:

  Analyse the different lifestyle choices that may result in poor health.

Remember, in your course exam the knowledge questions for the International Issues section will not refer to a particular country or issue. You will be expected to base your answer around your knowledge and understanding of the World Power or World Issue you have studied.

Remember, also, in your course exam that there will be no choice offered for skills-based questions and the context may be wide-ranging. These three questions are testing your skills and no knowledge is needed to answer the question.

When approaching an extended response question, keep in mind these common pitfalls:

What makes a poor extended response answer?

- One that does not answer the question, or tries to change the question being asked. This is sometimes called "turning a question".
- One that gives detailed description or explanation that is not relevant to the question.
- One that contains information which is out of date.
- One that **only** provides a list of facts with no development or analysis/evaluation.

What makes a good extended response answer?

- One that answers the question and only provides knowledge and understanding and analysis/evaluation that is **relevant** to the question.
- One that is aware of the different requirements of a 20-mark and 12-mark answer. A 20-mark answer should include greater skills of analysis and evaluation and be more structured than a 12-mark answer.
- One that uses **up-to-date, relevant** examples to illustrate your understanding of the question being asked.
- One that includes a range of points with detailed exemplification and explanation, and analysis/evaluation.
- For a 12-mark answer, one that includes knowledge/understanding and **either** analysis **or** evaluation. For a 20-mark response, one that includes knowledge/understanding, analysis, evaluation, a structure/line of argument and draws valid conclusions that address the question.

In the same way that you can practise what makes a good answer for extended response questions, you can do the same for source-based:

So, what makes a good source-based answer?

- A poor source-based answer doesn't make use of all the sources provided. To score well, be sure to refer to them all!
- Always link information across all of the sources.
- For the "objectivity" question, a vague statement such as "it is correct to an extent" will not get many marks. To be fully rewarded, make sure your answer includes a specific overall judgement on the statement.
- For the "conclusions" question, a weak response makes valid sub-conclusions but provides no evidence to support them, and/or fails to make an overall conclusion. Read your answer back to double check it draws a clear, supported overall conclusion.
- For the "reliability" question, an answer that provides vague and limited comment such as "Source A is reliable because it is up to date" is not enough. Make an effort to provide specific and detailed comment – and maximise your marks!

The most important thing is to keep calm, and don't panic!

You are now ready to tackle the exam questions.

Good luck!

Study Skills – what you need to know to pass exams!

General exam revision: 20 top tips

When preparing for exams, it is easy to feel unsure of where to start or how to revise. This guide to general exam revision provides a good starting place, and, as these are very general tips, they can be applied to all your exams.

1. Start revising in good time.

Don't leave revision until the last minute – this will make you panic and it will be difficult to learn. Make a revision timetable that counts down the weeks to go.

2. Work to a study plan.

Set up sessions of work spread through the weeks ahead. Make sure each session has a focus and a clear purpose. What will you study, when and why? Be realistic about what you can achieve in each session, and don't be afraid to adjust your plans as needed.

3. Make sure you know exactly when your exams are.

Get your exam dates from the SQA website and use the timetable builder tool to create your own exam schedule. You will also get a personalised timetable from your school, but this might not be until close to the exam period.

4. Make sure that you know the topics that make up each course.

Studying is easier if material is in manageable chunks – why not use the SQA topic headings or create your own from your class notes? Ask your teacher for help on this if you are not sure.

5. Break the chunks up into even smaller bits.

The small chunks should be easier to cope with. Remember that they fit together to make larger ideas. Even the process of chunking down will help!

6. Ask yourself these key questions for each course:

- Are all topics compulsory or are there choices?
- Which topics seem to come up time and time again?
- Which topics are your strongest and which are your weakest?

Use your answers to these questions to work out how much time you will need to spend revising each topic.

7. Make sure you know what to expect in the exam.

The subject-specific introduction to this book will help with this. Make sure you can answer these questions:

- How is the paper structured?
- How much time is there for each part of the exam?
- What types of question are involved? These will vary depending on the subject so read the subject-specific section carefully.

8. Past papers are a vital *revision tool!*

Use past papers to support your revision wherever possible. This book contains the answers and mark schemes too – refer to these carefully when checking your work. Using the mark scheme is useful; even if you don't manage to get all the marks available first time when you first practise, it helps you identify how to extend and develop your answers to get more marks next time – and of course, in the real exam.

9. Use study methods that work well for you.

People study and learn in different ways. Reading and looking at diagrams suits some students. Others prefer to listen and hear material – what about reading out loud or getting a friend or family member to do this for you? You could also record and play back material.

10. There are three tried and tested ways to make material stick in your long-term memory:

- Practising – e.g. rehearsal, repeating
- Organising – e.g. making drawings, lists, diagrams, tables, memory aids
- Elaborating – e.g. incorporating the material into a story or an imagined journey

11. Learn actively.

Most people prefer to learn actively – for example, making notes, highlighting, redrawing and redrafting, making up memory aids, or writing past paper answers. A good way to stay engaged and inspired is to mix and match these methods – find the combination that best suits you. This is likely to vary depending on the topic or subject.

12. Be an expert.

Be sure to have a few areas in which you feel you are an expert. This often works because at least some of them will come up, which can boost confidence.

13. Try some visual methods.

Use symbols, diagrams, charts, flashcards, post-it notes etc. Don't forget – the brain takes in chunked images more easily than loads of text.

14. Remember – practice makes perfect.

Work on difficult areas again and again. Look and read – then test yourself. You cannot do this too much.

15. Try past papers against the clock.

Practise writing answers in a set time. This is a good habit from the start but is especially important when you get closer to exam time.

16. Collaborate with friends.

Test each other and talk about the material – this can really help. Two brains are better than one! It is amazing how talking about a problem can help you solve it.

17. Know your weaknesses.

Ask your teacher for help to identify what you don't know. Try to do this as early as possible. If you are having trouble, it is probably with a difficult topic, so your teacher will already be aware of this – most students will find it tough.

18. Have your materials organised and ready.

Know what is needed for each exam:

- Do you need a calculator or a ruler?
- Should you have pencils as well as pens?
- Will you need water or paper tissues?

19. Make full use of school resources.

Find out what support is on offer:

- Are there study classes available?
- When is the library open?
- When is the best time to ask for extra help?
- Can you borrow textbooks, study guides, past papers, etc.?
- Is school open for Easter revision?

20. Keep fit and healthy!

Try to stick to a routine as much as possible, including with sleep. If you are tired, sluggish or dehydrated, it is difficult to see how concentration is even possible. Combine study with relaxation, drink plenty of water, eat sensibly, and get fresh air and exercise – all these things will help more than you could imagine. Good luck!

HIGHER

2018

National
Qualifications
2018

X749/76/11

Modern Studies

WEDNESDAY, 9 MAY
9:00 AM — 11:15 AM

Total marks — 60

SECTION 1 — DEMOCRACY IN SCOTLAND AND THE UNITED KINGDOM — 20 marks

Attempt **EITHER** question 1(a) **OR** 1(b) **AND** question 2

SECTION 2 — SOCIAL ISSUES IN THE UNITED KINGDOM — 20 marks
Part A Social inequality in the United Kingdom
Part B Crime and the law in the United Kingdom

Attempt **EITHER** question 3(a) **OR** 3(b) **OR** 3(c) **OR** 3(d) **AND** question 4

SECTION 3 — INTERNATIONAL ISSUES — 20 marks
Part A World powers
Part B World issues

Attempt **EITHER** question 5(a) **OR** 5(b) **OR** 5(c) **OR** 5(d)

Write your answers clearly in the answer booklet provided. In the answer booklet you must clearly identify the question number you are attempting.

Use **blue** or **black** ink.

Before leaving the examination room you must give your answer booklet to the Invigilator; if you do not, you may lose all the marks for this paper.

MARKS

SECTION 1 — DEMOCRACY IN SCOTLAND AND THE UNITED KINGDOM — 20 marks

Attempt **EITHER** question 1 (a) **OR** 1 (b) **AND** question 2

Question 1

(a) Analyse the potential impact of leaving the European Union.

You should refer to issues affecting Scotland **or** the United Kingdom **or** both in your answer. **12**

OR

(b) Analyse the influence of the media on voting behaviour.

You should refer to voting behaviour in Scotland **or** the United Kingdom **or** both in your answer. **12**

[Turn over for next question

DO NOT WRITE ON THIS PAGE

Question 2

Study Sources A, B and C and then attempt the question that follows.

Source A

The role of committees — 'Parliament at work'

Committees are central to the work of the Scottish Parliament. The job of the committees is vital as the Scottish Parliament has no second chamber (unlike the UK Parliament). They have three broad roles:

- to scrutinise legislation and to hold the Scottish Government (currently the SNP) to account for its actions
- to introduce legislation (ie new laws)
- to conduct inquiries, gather evidence and produce reports into matters within their remit (eg recent inquiries into education by the Education and Skills Committee).

It is in these three areas that the success of the Scottish Parliament's committees is judged.

The membership of the committees is made up of MSPs from every party, with Committee Conveners, who chair meetings and set agendas, being drawn from different parties. Membership reflects the balance of power in parliament — some argue that this builds in a pro-government bias. Every piece of legislation that comes out of Holyrood comes under the scrutiny of one or more of the Scottish Parliament's committees.

Committees often meet in public and can do so anywhere in Scotland, not just inside parliament. In fact, most committees allow the general public to attend and most committee meetings are streamed live on the Scottish Parliament website. Committees have managed to amend government legislation on hundreds of occasions. Committees also have the power to introduce their own legislation ie a Committee Bill.

The Public Petitions Committee (PPC) is the main way for members of the public to influence policy. It is often called the jewel in Holyrood's crown with the general public believing the PPC to be a credit to our democracy. A petition to scrap the Offensive Behaviour at Football Act received nearly 10,000 signatures however the government wasn't forced to take action by this. In Parliamentary Session 4 (2011–2016), 170 petitions were considered by the PPC. The equivalent committee in the Welsh Assembly considered 356 petitions in that time.

Adapted from a variety of news sources.

Source B

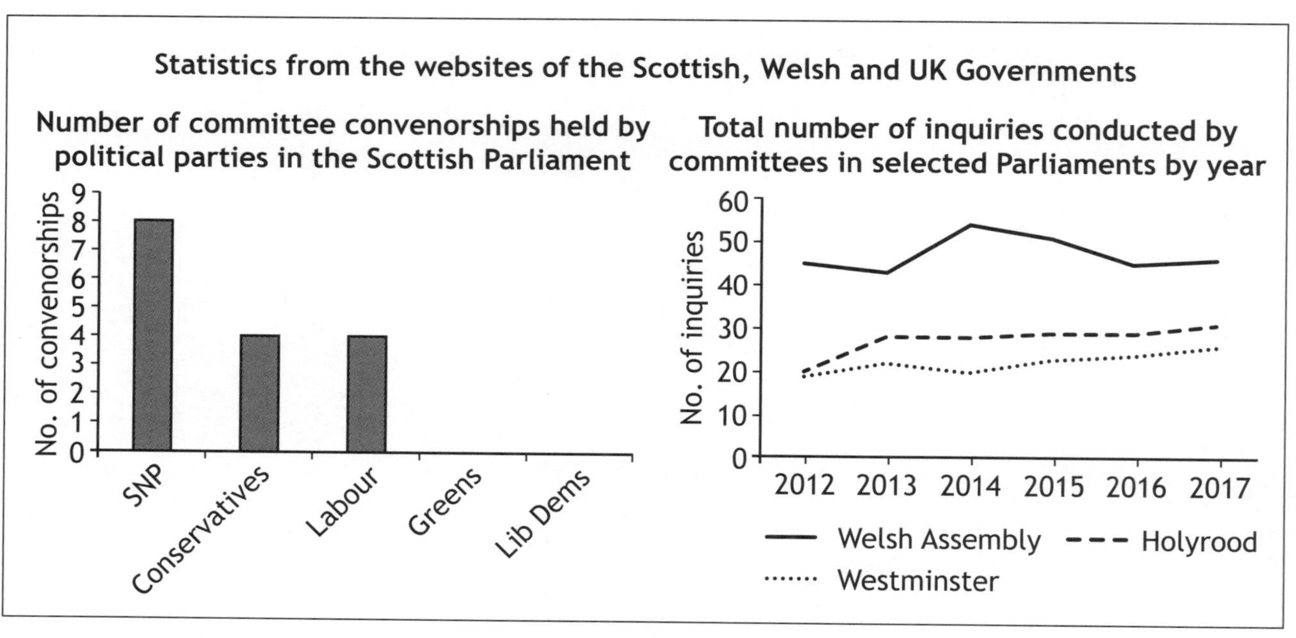

Question 2 (continued)

MARKS

Source B (continued)

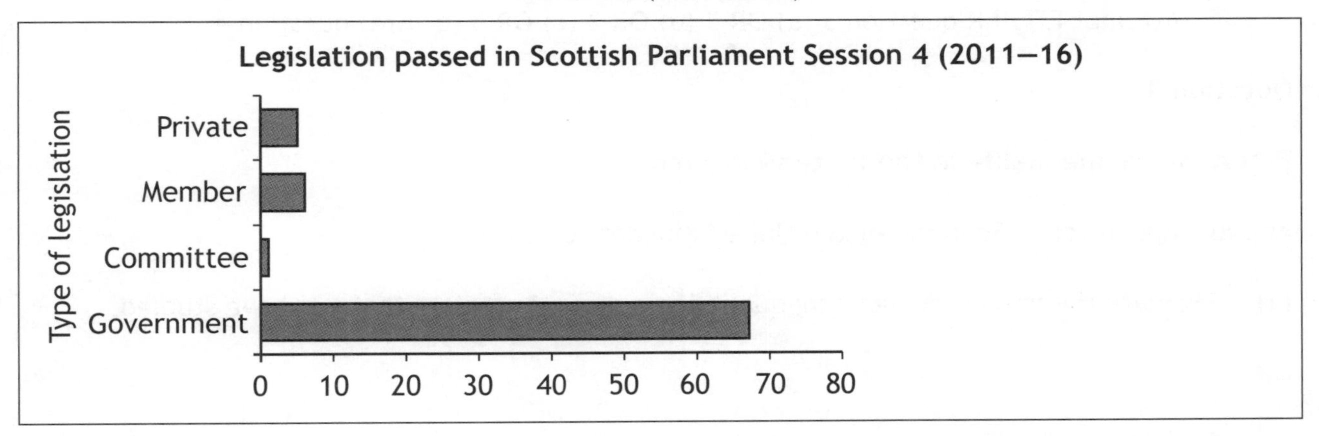

Source C

Public attitude survey on the Scottish Parliament

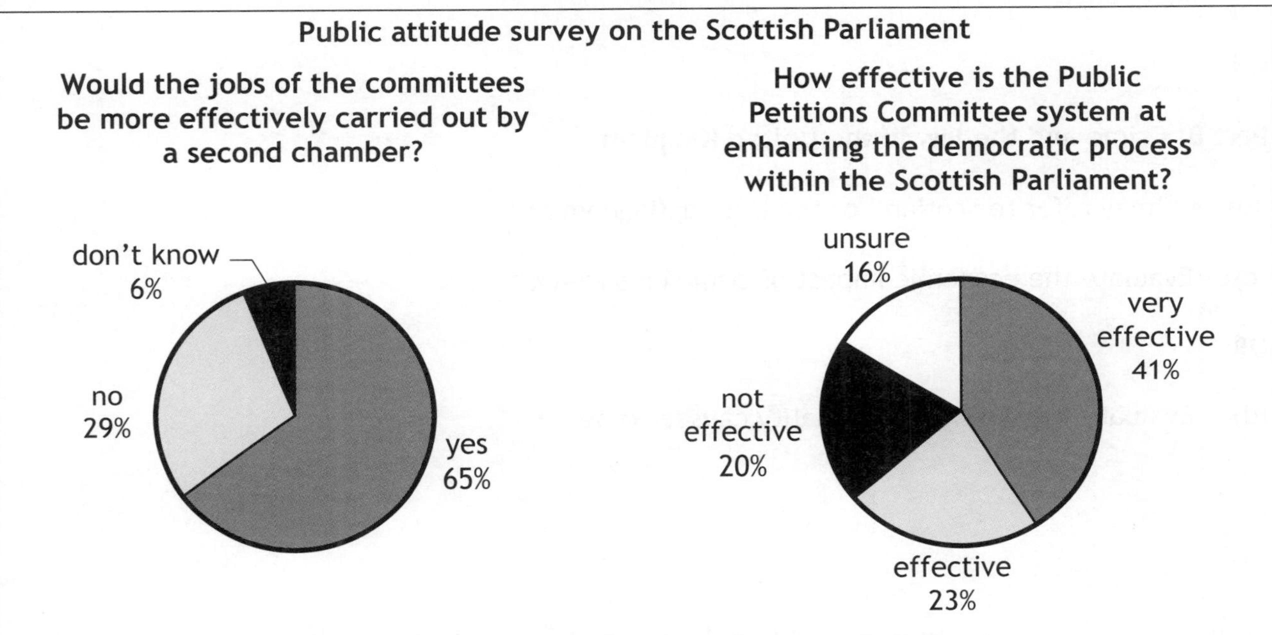

Statement: 'The committee system must do better'

The committee system — intended to be the engine room of Scottish parliamentary democracy — has been criticised for failing in a crucial function: to introduce legislation.

Some would also argue that the committee system is not fully independent of government as their membership reflects the distribution of party power in parliament. The dominance of the SNP means their MSPs make up a large proportion of membership in each committee eg five of the eleven members of the Education and Skills Committee are from the SNP, including the Convenor.

To their credit, committees engage in short and 'snappy' inquiries with the potential to provide timely advice to government. However, Scottish Parliamentary committees seem to be lacking the resources and time to conduct inquiries at the same rate as other comparable parliaments, such as the Welsh Assembly. However, committee inquiries can compel witnesses, including Scottish Government Ministers, to attend or provide written evidence. Failure to do so is a criminal offence.

Survey data and statement from a blog by a Professor of Politics at a Scottish University.

Answer the following question, using **only** the information in Sources A, B and C on *Page four* and above.

To what extent is it accurate to state that the Scottish Parliament's committees fulfil their roles effectively?

In your answer, you may wish to evaluate the reliability of the sources. 8

MARKS

SECTION 2 — SOCIAL ISSUES IN THE UNITED KINGDOM — 20 marks

Attempt **EITHER** question 3 (a) **OR** 3 (b) **OR** 3 (c) **OR** 3 (d) **AND** question 4

Question 3

Part A: Social inequality in the United Kingdom

Answers may refer to Scotland **or** the United Kingdom **or** both.

(a) Evaluate the impact of social inequality on a group in society that you have studied. **12**

OR

(b) Evaluate the view that government should be responsible for tackling social inequality. **12**

OR

Part B: Crime and the law in the United Kingdom

Answers may refer to Scotland **or** the United Kingdom **or** both.

(c) Evaluate the economic impact of crime on society. **12**

OR

(d) Evaluate the view that inequality causes crime. **12**

[Turn over for next question

DO NOT WRITE ON THIS PAGE

Question 4

Study Sources A, B and C then attempt the question that follows.

Source A

British prisons

Crime rates in Britain are falling, however the prison population remains high and is nearly double that of 20 years ago. Recent reductions in prison staff have meant that it is more difficult for staff to control the large prison population. Britain now has the largest prison population in Western Europe at 93,665, which is nearly 20,000 higher than France and 30,000 more than Germany.

In England and Wales 60% of prisons accommodate more prisoners than their Certified Normal Accommodation (CNA). CNA is calculated by the Prison Service and represents the good, decent standard of accommodation that it aims to provide to all prisoners. As a consequence of overcrowding some prisons are forced to 'double-up' prisoners by housing two in cells designed for one. In 2014–15, 21,755 people were held in overcrowded accommodation, with the majority of these doubling-up in cells.

Frances Crook, chief executive of the Howard League for Penal Reform, has said that 'without enough staff to keep people safe, prisons are increasingly providing restricted regimes, under which prisoners are locked in their cells for up to 23 hours a day.' Human Rights groups have claimed that being locked up for 23 hours a day is degrading and that it reduces the rehabilitation services offered in prison. They also claim that prisons are unable to provide adequate healthcare and that the mental health of prisoners is negatively affected. Thameside prison was recently criticised by inspectors for locking up 60% of prisoners for 23 hours a day due to the rising level of gang violence within the prison.

Prison staff have reported that there is a growing level of violence and rioting in prisons which they are not able to control. In 2013, the Prison Service's riot squad in England and Wales was called out 203 times (129 times in 2012). In 2016, Birmingham prison faced a 12-hour riot where 600 prisoners took over 4 wings of the prison.

This picture of overcrowding continues in Scotland with Barlinnie prison in recent times operating at 20% above its design capacity. Further to this, in Scotland's only women's prison (Cornton Vale) some prisoners in the recent past have been forced to use their sinks as toilets due to night-time security arrangements. Prisoners are faced with waits of more than an hour before being allowed to use the toilet, in what inspectors have described as a significant breach of human dignity.

Source B

Selected statistics on prison populations in England and Wales

Prison	No. of prisoners	Certified Normal Accommodation (CNA)
Doncaster	1,115	738
Liverpool	1,097	1,101
Pentonville	1,238	906
Thameside	1,223	932
Wormwood Scrubs	1,231	1,156
Total	**84,069**	**74,703**

Question 4 (continued) **MARKS**

Source B (continued)

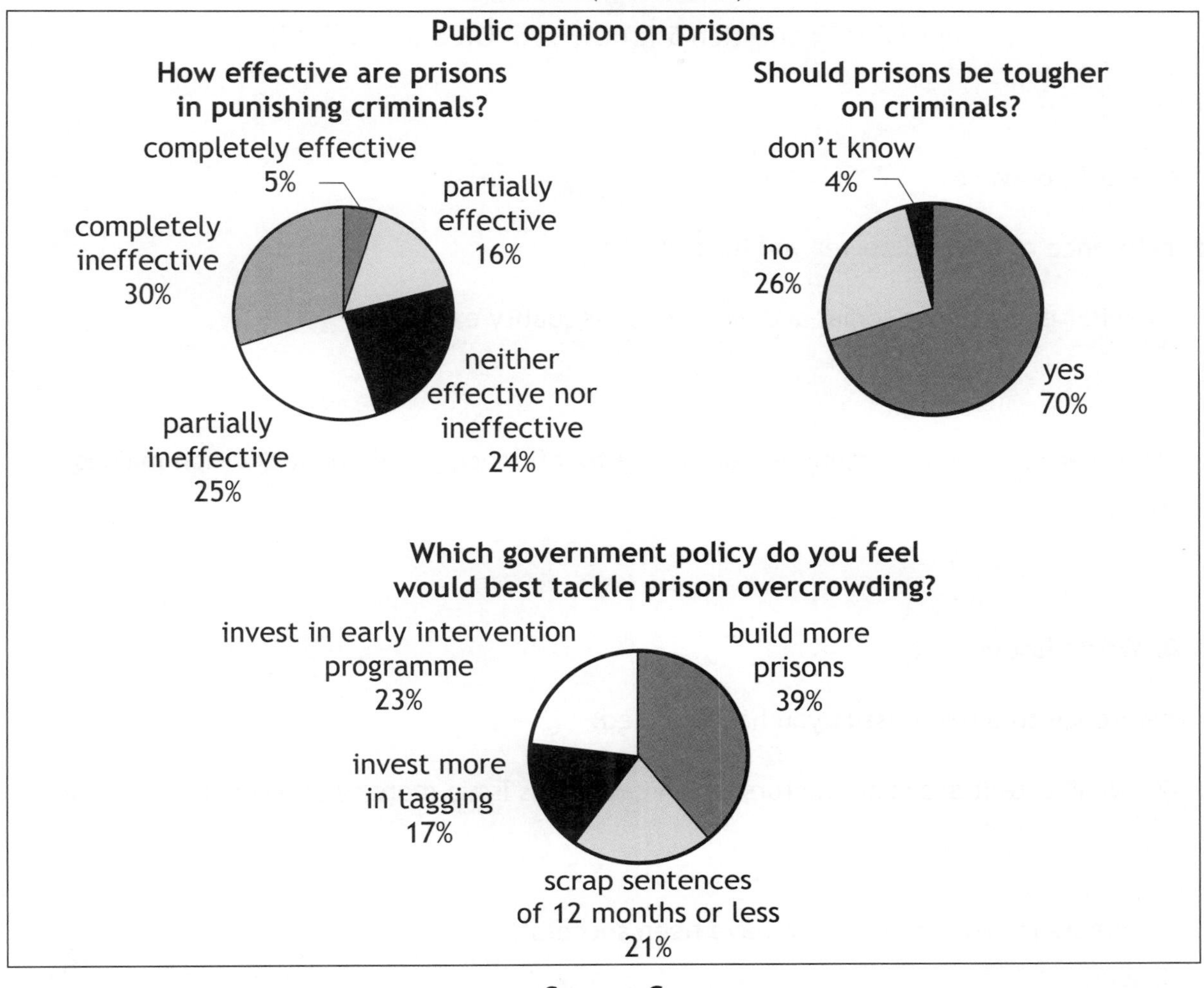

Source C

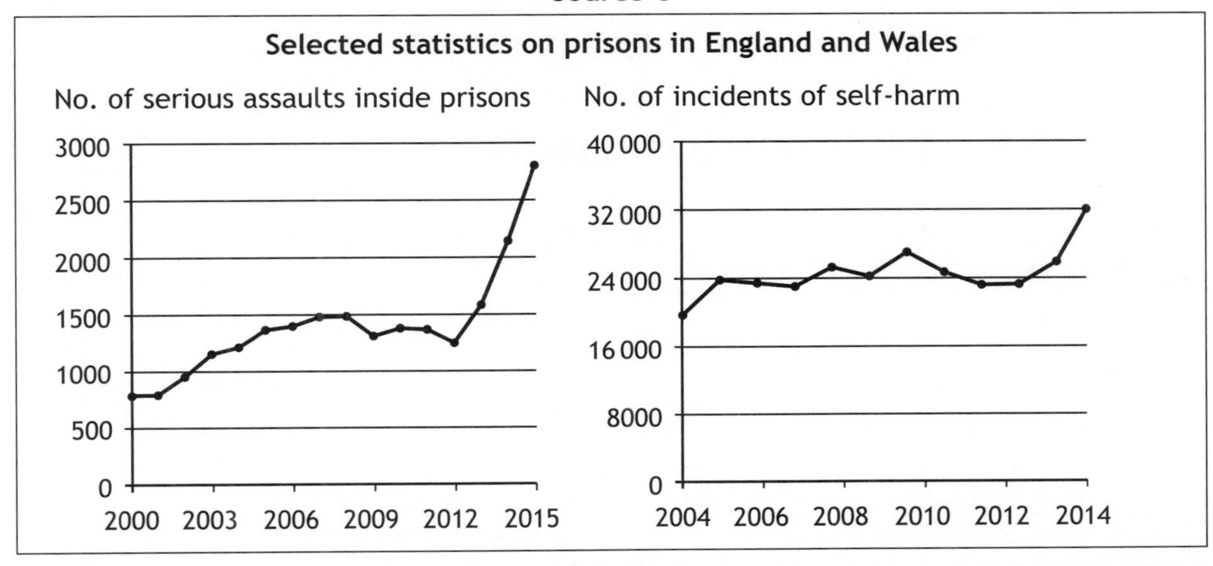

Attempt the following question, using **only** the information in Sources A, B and C on *Page eight* and above.

What conclusions can be drawn about overcrowding in British prisons?

You must draw conclusions about:

- overcrowding and the living conditions of prisoners
- overcrowding and safety in prisons.

You should provide an overall conclusion about the extent of overcrowding in British prisons. **8**

[Turn over

MARKS

SECTION 3 — INTERNATIONAL ISSUES — 20 marks

Attempt **EITHER** question 5 (a) **OR** 5 (b) **OR** 5 (c) **OR** 5 (d)

Question 5

Part A: World powers

With reference to a world power you have studied:

(a) To what extent does social and economic inequality exist? **20**

OR

(b) There are limited opportunities for people to influence government decision making. Discuss. **20**

OR

Part B: World issues

With reference to a world issue you have studied:

(c) To what extent are some factors which cause this issue more important than others? **20**

OR

(d) Attempts to resolve this issue have been successful. Discuss. **20**

[END OF QUESTION PAPER]

HIGHER

2018 Specimen Question Paper

S849/76/11

Modern Studies
Paper 1

Date — Not applicable

Duration — 1 hour 45 minutes

Total marks — 52

SECTION 1 — DEMOCRACY IN SCOTLAND AND THE UNITED KINGDOM — 20 marks

Attempt **ONE** question from 1(a) **OR** 1(b) **OR** 1(c)

SECTION 2 — SOCIAL ISSUES IN THE UNITED KINGDOM — 20 marks

Part A Social inequality

Part B Crime and the law

Attempt **ONE** question from 2(a) **OR** 2(b) **OR** 2(c) **OR** 2(d)

SECTION 3 — INTERNATIONAL ISSUES — 12 marks

Part C World powers

Part D World issues

Attempt **ONE** question from 3(a) **OR** 3(b) **OR** 3(c) **OR** 3(d)

Write your answers clearly in the answer booklet provided. In the answer booklet you must clearly identify the question number you are attempting.

Use **blue** or **black** ink.

Before leaving the examination room you must give your answer booklet to the Invigilator; if you do not, you may lose all the marks for this paper.

MARKS

SECTION 1 — DEMOCRACY IN SCOTLAND AND THE UNITED KINGDOM — 20 marks

Attempt **ONE** question from 1 (a) **OR** 1 (b) **OR** 1 (c)

Question 1

(a) To what extent is age the most influential factor on voting behaviour?

You should refer to Scotland **or** the United Kingdom **or** both in your answer. **20**

OR

(b) To what extent will leaving the European Union have positive implications for the United Kingdom?

You should refer to Scotland **or** the United Kingdom **or** both in your answer. **20**

OR

(c) To what extent can parliamentary representatives effectively check the powers of the government?

You should refer to Scotland **or** the United Kingdom **or** both in your answer. **20**

MARKS

SECTION 2 — SOCIAL ISSUES IN THE UNITED KINGDOM — 20 marks

Attempt **ONE** question from 2 (a) **OR** 2 (b) **OR** 2 (c) **OR** 2 (d)

Question 2

Part A: Social inequality

Answers may refer to Scotland **or** the United Kingdom **or** both.

(a) There are many causes of income and wealth inequality.
Discuss. **20**

OR

(b) Government measures have failed to reduce inequalities.
Discuss. **20**

OR

Part B: Crime and the law

Answers may refer to Scotland **or** the United Kingdom **or** both.

(c) There are many causes of crime.
Discuss. **20**

OR

(d) Non-custodial responses to crime have failed.
Discuss. **20**

[Turn over

MARKS

SECTION 3 — INTERNATIONAL ISSUES — 12 marks

Attempt **ONE** question from 3 (a) **OR** 3 (b) **OR** 3 (c) **OR** 3 (d)

Question 3

Part A: World powers

With reference to a world power you have studied:

(a) Analyse the opportunities that exist for people to influence decision making. **12**

OR

(b) Evaluate the success of the government in tackling socio-economic inequality. **12**

OR

Part B: World issues

With reference to a world issue you have studied:

(c) Analyse the attempts of international organisations to tackle the issue. **12**

OR

(d) Evaluate the impact of the issue on individuals, families and communities. **12**

[END OF SPECIMEN QUESTION PAPER]

H

National
Qualifications
SPECIMEN ONLY

S849/76/12

Modern Studies
Paper 2

Date — Not applicable

Duration — 1 hour 15 minutes

Total marks — 28

Attempt **ALL** questions

Write your answers clearly in the answer booklet provided. In the answer booklet you must clearly identify the question number you are attempting.

Use **blue** or **black** ink.

Before leaving the examination room you must give your answer booklet to the Invigilator; if you do not, you may lose all the marks for this paper.

Total marks — 28

Attempt ALL questions

Question 1

Study Sources A, B and C then attempt the question that follows.

Source A

Scottish independence referendum

The Scottish independence referendum was notable for several reasons. First of all it gave the vote to 16 and 17 year olds for the first time. Also because, if successful, it would have led to the breakup of the 300 year old United Kingdom. Finally, it was notable for the high level of political debate and interest within Scotland during the campaign.

Across all 32 council areas in Scotland, 85% of voters participated and when all of the votes had been counted, the result was clear: Scotland had chosen to remain part of the United Kingdom by a margin of 55% to 45%. Over 3·6 million votes were cast. Just over 2 million voters chose to place their X in the NO box in response to the question "Should Scotland be an Independent Country?"

In the days and weeks that followed, political scientists tried to provide reasons why people voted the way they did. Although the average turnout was 85%, this figure varied greatly between areas with different socio-economic profiles. Of the 32 Scottish council areas, four voted YES. What is striking is that each of these four areas had high levels of poverty and social deprivation.

The influence of age as a factor was considered by many, particularly as 16 and 17 year olds were allowed to vote. However, it may have been the decisions of older voters rather than their younger counterparts that were important, particularly as older voters are more likely to turn out in higher numbers. Female voters seemed to be swayed more by the NO campaign's arguments.

Result and turnout

Scottish independence referendum (selected regions)

Region	Yes (%)	Turnout (%)
Aberdeen City	41·4	81·7
Aberdeenshire	39·6	87·2
Dundee City	57·4	78·8
East Dunbartonshire	38·8	91
East Renfrewshire	36·8	90·4
Edinburgh	38·9	84·4
Glasgow	53·5	75
North Lanarkshire	51·1	84·4
Perth and Kinross	39·8	86·9
West Dunbartonshire	54	87·9

Question 1 (continued)

Source B

How did you vote in the Scottish independence referendum?

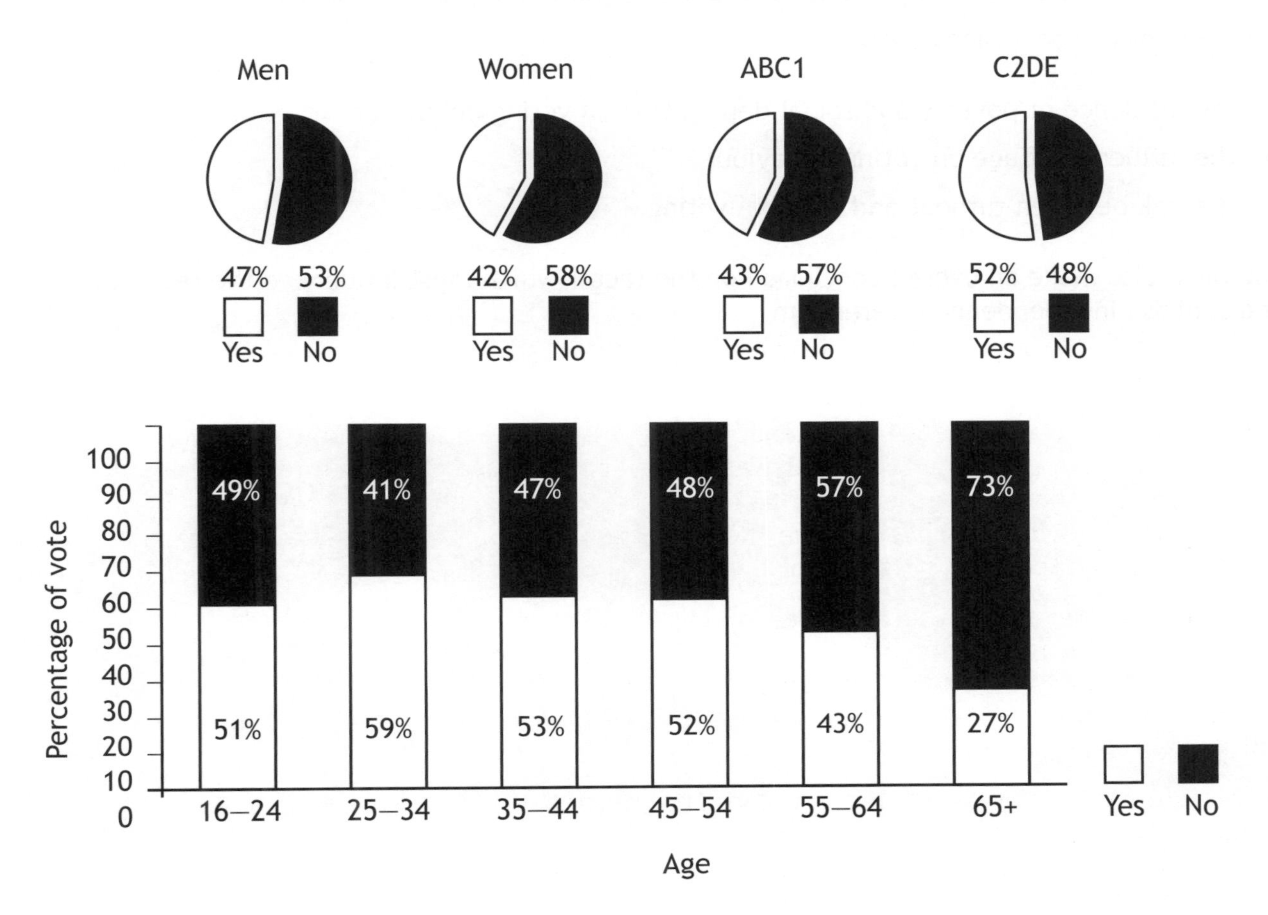

Source C

Social and economic indicators (selected regions)

	Employment rate (%)	Unemployment rate (%)	% of child poverty in region
Aberdeen City	77·3	1·4	18
Aberdeenshire	78·6	0·6	14
Dundee City	61·4	4·4	28
East Dunbartonshire	77·1	1·4	13
East Renfrewshire	74·2	1·4	15
Edinburgh	71·7	2·2	21
Glasgow	63·3	4·2	33
North Lanarkshire	70·2	3·8	25
Perth and Kinross	75·3	1·6	17
West Dunbartonshire	65·2	4·3	25

MARKS

Attempt the following question, using only the information in Sources A, B and C on *Pages two* and *three*.

Question 1 (continued)

What conclusions can be drawn about the result of the Scottish independence referendum?

You must draw conclusions about:

- the influence of poverty and social deprivation on voting behaviour
- the influence of age on voting behaviour
- the link between turnout and regional voting.

You must also make an overall conclusion on the factor which **most** influenced the result of the Scottish independence referendum. **10**

Question 2

Study Sources A, B and C then attempt the question that follows.

Source A

Russia's 'foreign agents'

In 2012 Russia's parliament adopted a law that required campaign groups to register as 'foreign agents' with the Ministry of Justice if they engaged in 'political activity' and received foreign funding. The definition of political activity under the law is so broad and vague that it covered almost all campaign groups in Russia.

Russian authorities arrested and harassed activists, blocked independent online media and proposed measures that would further stifle free expression. More recently pro-government media published material blaming the Government of Ukraine for the ongoing civil war in that country, trying to deflect attention away from Russia's invasion and occupation of Crimea.

In Russia 'foreign agent' is interpreted as 'spy' or 'traitor'. The groups campaigning for political freedoms were in no doubt that the law aimed to demonise them, and to turn the public against them. Russia's many human rights groups boycotted the law, calling it 'slanderous'. Many of them have now been forced to disband and many of their leaders have been prosecuted for refusing to register as a foreign agent. In the past such individuals may have faced the death sentence but Russia has not executed anyone since 1996.

In August 2013, four organisations challenged the law in Russia's Constitutional Court. On 8 April 2014 the court upheld the law, ruling that the term 'foreign agent' had no negative connotations, therefore its use was 'not intended to persecute or discredit' anyone. The court also found that labelling campaign groups as foreign agents was in the interests of state security and did not affect the right to protest. The ruling has been heavily criticised by many foreign governments.

[Turn over

MARKS

Question 2 (continued)

Source B

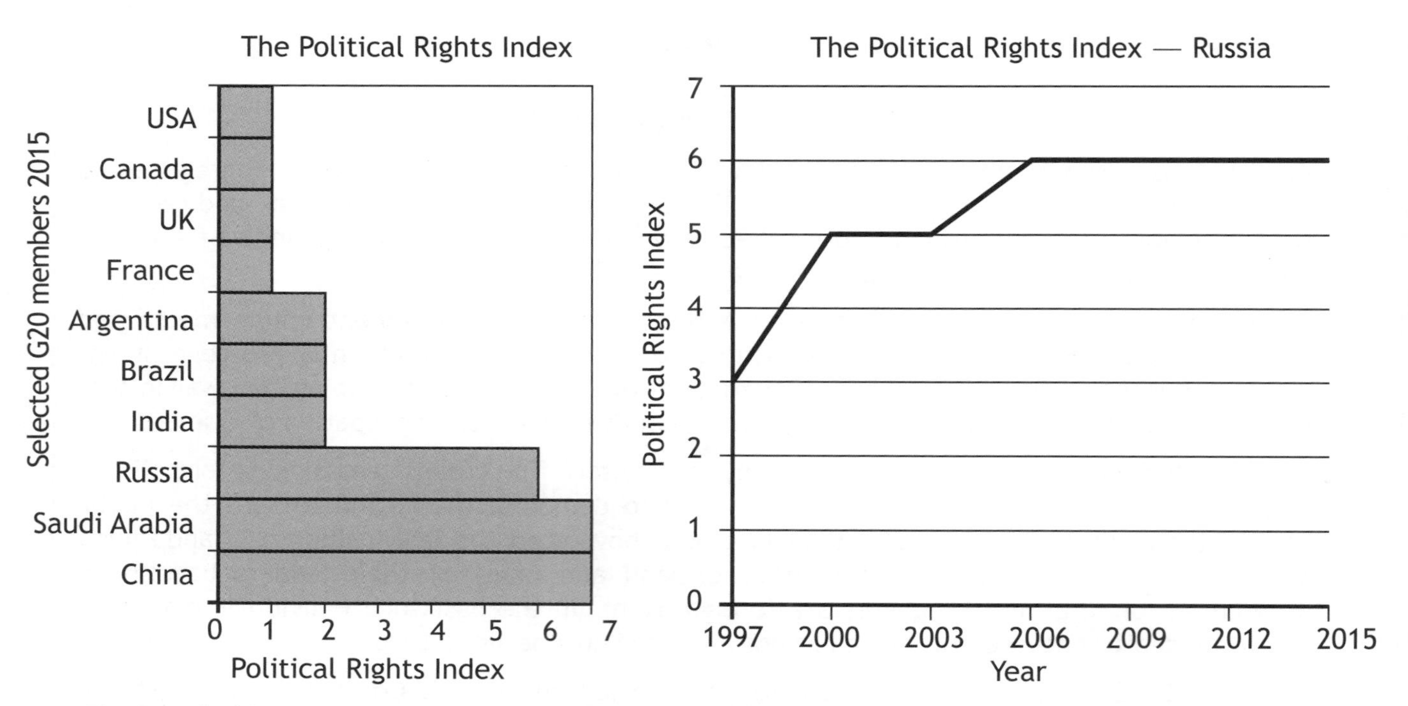

(7 = People have very weak political rights, 1 = People have very strong political rights)

Source C

Annual report 2014

"There have been fewer complaints from Russians over human rights violations", Government spokesman Vladimir Lukin said in his annual report. He said that more than half of the complaints he had received last year were about violations of civil rights and freedoms. The number of complaints concerning political rights was relatively small, and complaints about religious freedoms and freedom of conscience decreased by 10%.

In 2014, Mr Lukin's offices received 24,000 complaints; in 2012 the figure was 58,000. Many people were worried about violations of their personal rights, others complained about unfair court rulings; more than half of the letters (56%) were complaints about the courts and nearly one-quarter of the complaints were about abuses by the police or prison staff. As for political complaints, they accounted for 2% of the total. Lukin also praised a recent report by the European Union which congratulated Russia on its expansion of jury trials across Russia and its suspension of the death penalty.

As he submitted his report to President Vladimir Putin, Lukin brought up the issue of mass inspections of human rights groups, launched in recent weeks. Lukin assured the journalists that political campaign groups had nothing to fear and that their right to protest was protected by Russian law.

Attempt the following question, using only the information in Sources A, B and C on *Page five* and above.

To what extent is it accurate to state that Russia effectively protects the rights of its citizens? **10**

Question 3

Study Sources A, B and C then attempt the question that follows.

Source A

Interview with British jihadi in Syria

What made you leave the UK? What was the deciding factor?
To come to Syria. To leave *dar al kufr* [the land of disbelievers].

Why are you out in Syria?
To spread the religion of Allah and to help Muslims. I can speak Arabic and English. That's like my only skill. I've spent efforts to take down the Syrian government. That's all I want to say.

Have you joined Isis?
I'm not Isis, but I believe in the Sharia. I believe we should follow Islam how the first Muslims did. I also think that whatever I say, the media will probably freestyle with it and make up more nicknames for me as a result of the void they have in their lives.

What do you think about Isis? Can you give us an insight into what's going on in Syria with Isis? They've recently released a video saying they'll attack the UK — what are your thoughts on that?
I'm doing my own thing. I don't focus that much on what Isis does. Also this may sound strange but this is genuinely the first time someone's told me they threatened to attack the UK, which is probably a bit embarrassing, seeing as I'm in Syria and you'd expect I'd hear these things. If Britain stopped bombing Muslims in Syria the Muslims in Syria would stop attacking them. Is that hard to understand?

Source: The Independent, *'Jihadi Jack' Letts interview: Former Oxford schoolboy calls on British people to convert to Islam as he brands David Cameron an 'evil creature'* by Shebab Khan, published 30 January 2016.

Source B

Public opinion survey: issues facing Britain
What do you see as the biggest issue facing the UK today?

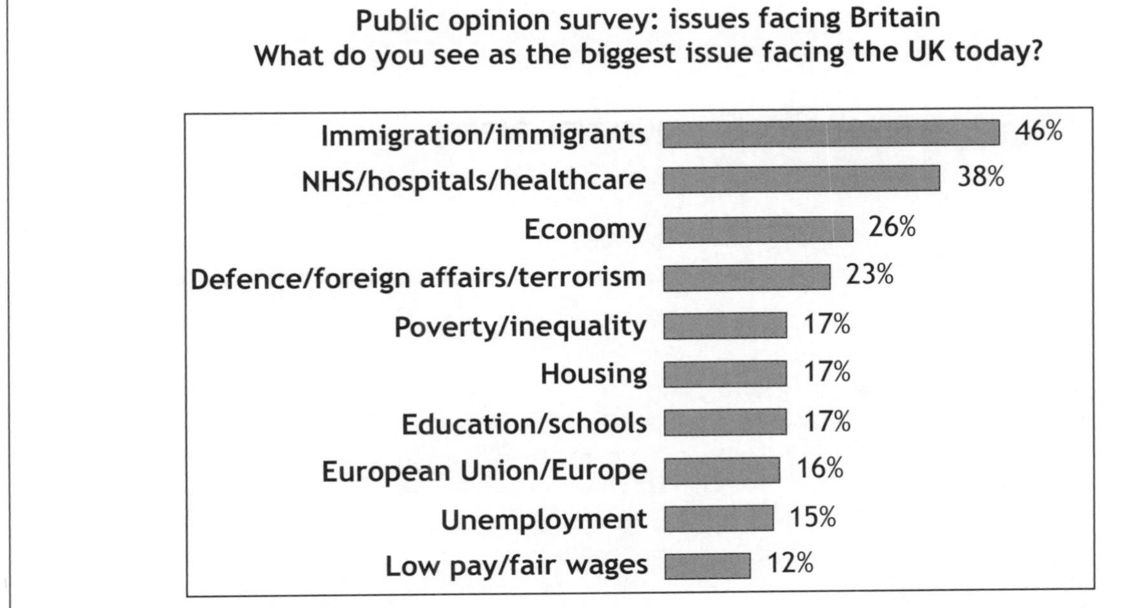

Source: Ipsos MORI interviewed a representative quota sample of 1,011 adults aged 18+ across Great Britain, 7–20 January 2016.

MARKS

Question 3 (continued)

Source C

Channel 4 website

Source: Channel 4 News website, *"Do we know why we are in Afghanistan?"* by Jon Snow, published 28 July 2009.

Attempt the following question, using only the information in Sources A, B and C on *Page seven* and above.

To what extent are Sources A, B and C reliable?

You must provide an overall conclusion on the most reliable source of information. **8**

[END OF SPECIMEN QUESTION PAPER]

HIGHER

2019

X849/76/11

Modern Studies
Paper 1

WEDNESDAY, 1 MAY

9:00 AM – 10:45 AM

Total marks — 52

SECTION 1 — DEMOCRACY IN SCOTLAND AND THE UNITED KINGDOM — 20 marks

Attempt **ONE** question from 1(a) **OR** 1(b) **OR** 1(c).

SECTION 2 — SOCIAL ISSUES IN THE UNITED KINGDOM — 12 marks

Part A Social inequality

Part B Crime and the law

Attempt **ONE** question from 2(a) **OR** 2(b) **OR** 2(c) **OR** 2(d).

SECTION 3 — INTERNATIONAL ISSUES — 20 marks

Part C World powers

Part D World issues

Attempt **ONE** question from 3(a) **OR** 3(b) **OR** 3(c) **OR** 3(d).

Write your answers clearly in the answer booklet provided. In the answer booklet you must clearly identify the question number you are attempting.

Use **blue** or **black** ink.

Before leaving the examination room you must give your answer booklet to the Invigilator; if you do not, you may lose all the marks for this paper.

MARKS

SECTION 1 — DEMOCRACY IN SCOTLAND AND THE UNITED KINGDOM — 20 marks

Attempt **ONE** question from 1(a) **OR** 1(b) **OR** 1(c)

Question 1

(a) There are many different views about the most effective way to govern Scotland.

Discuss.

You should refer to Scotland **or** the United Kingdom **or** both in your answer. **20**

OR

(b) Parliament has had little success in holding the government to account.

Discuss.

You should refer to Scotland **or** the United Kingdom **or** both in your answer. **20**

OR

(c) Some pressure groups, and the methods they use, are more successful than others.

Discuss.

You should refer to Scotland **or** the United Kingdom **or** both in your answer. **20**

MARKS

SECTION 2 — SOCIAL ISSUES IN THE UNITED KINGDOM — 12 marks

Attempt **ONE** question from 2(a) **OR** 2(b) **OR** 2(c) **OR** 2(d)

Question 2

Part A: Social inequality

Answers may refer to Scotland **or** the United Kingdom **or** both.

(a) Analyse the effect of inequality on **a group** in society. **12**

OR

(b) Evaluate the effectiveness of government policies in tackling inequalities. **12**

OR

Part B: Crime and the law

Answers may refer to Scotland **or** the United Kingdom **or** both.

(c) Analyse the ways in which **victims** of crime are affected. **12**

OR

(d) Evaluate the effectiveness of non-custodial responses to crime. **12**

[Turn over

MARKS

SECTION 3 — INTERNATIONAL ISSUES — 20 marks

Attempt **ONE** question from 3(a) **OR** 3(b) **OR** 3(c) **OR** 3(d)

Question 3

Part C: World powers

With reference to a world power you have studied

(a) to what extent is government decision-making dominated by one branch of government or political institution? **20**

OR

(b) to what extent does a world power that you have studied have international influence? **20**

OR

Part D: World issues

With reference to a world issue you have studied

(c) to what extent does the issue have an effect on the wider international community? **20**

OR

(d) to what extent has the response by individual countries to this issue been effective? **20**

[END OF QUESTION PAPER]

H

National
Qualifications
2019

X849/76/12

Modern Studies
Paper 2

WEDNESDAY, 1 MAY

11:15 AM – 12:30 PM

Total marks — 28

Attempt **ALL** questions

Write your answers clearly in the answer booklet provided. In the answer booklet you must clearly identify the question number you are attempting.

Use **blue** or **black** ink.

Before leaving the examination room you must give your answer booklet to the Invigilator; if you do not, you may lose all the marks for this paper.

[OPEN OUT]

DO NOT WRITE ON THIS PAGE

Total marks — 28

Attempt **ALL** questions

Question 1

Study Sources A, B and C then attempt the question that follows.

Source A

Minimum unit pricing for alcohol — one year on

On the 1st of May 2018 Scotland became the first country in the world to implement a minimum unit price for alcohol (MUP). The minimum price for alcohol set a floor price for a unit of alcohol at 50p. Drinks like strong white cider, super strength lager and own brand vodka were most affected. It was once possible to buy a 3 litre bottle of strong cider with 22 units of alcohol in it for £3·99 but the same cider now costs £11. The legislation includes a 'sunset clause', meaning that it will expire after six years unless the Scottish Parliament passes an order to extend it. Other UK countries have yet to introduce MUP but are looking to introduce it in the near future.

Analysis of current consumption patterns shows that, within the Scottish population, 14·9% do not drink, 60·5% are moderate drinkers, 19·1% are hazardous drinkers and 5·5% are harmful drinkers. Men still drink more alcohol than women whereas women tend to drink more expensive alcoholic beverages such as wines and gin that MUP doesn't affect. On average, drinkers who live in poverty used to purchase approximately 500 units of alcohol per year, for less than 50p per unit, however after a year of MUP this figure has decreased. Interestingly, this has not been the case with those in better off socio-economic groups (A and B). A critic of MUP argued, 'it is not the prosecco drinking well-to-do in society that minimum pricing affects, it is the everyday person trying to buy a drink that he or she can afford.'

A main aim of MUP is to tackle the social issues associated with alcohol. 60% of young offenders were drunk at the time of their offence, often having consumed strong tonic wine which is priced above 50p per unit. High tariff crimes such as murder and violence show a small decrease in recent years but it is debatable whether this has any relation to MUP. Unexpectedly, MUP may actually be causing a rise in crime as supermarkets have reported an increase in the theft of strong alcohol. With regards to alcohol related ill health, MUP aims to make dangerous 'binge drinking' more expensive. As 'binge drinking' is a major cause of hospitalisation, it is hoped that alcohol-related ill health will be reduced. Medical experts warn that one 'binge drinking' session is more damaging to the liver than drinking moderately numerous times during the week. The idea that MUP would be the next 'smoking ban' in terms of major health benefits has yet to materialise but signs are looking positive for the future.

Public survey: What effect has MUP had on your alcohol consumption level?

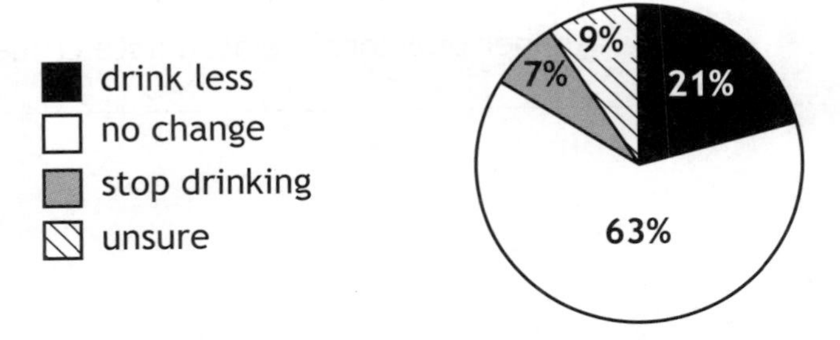

Question 1 (continued)

Source B

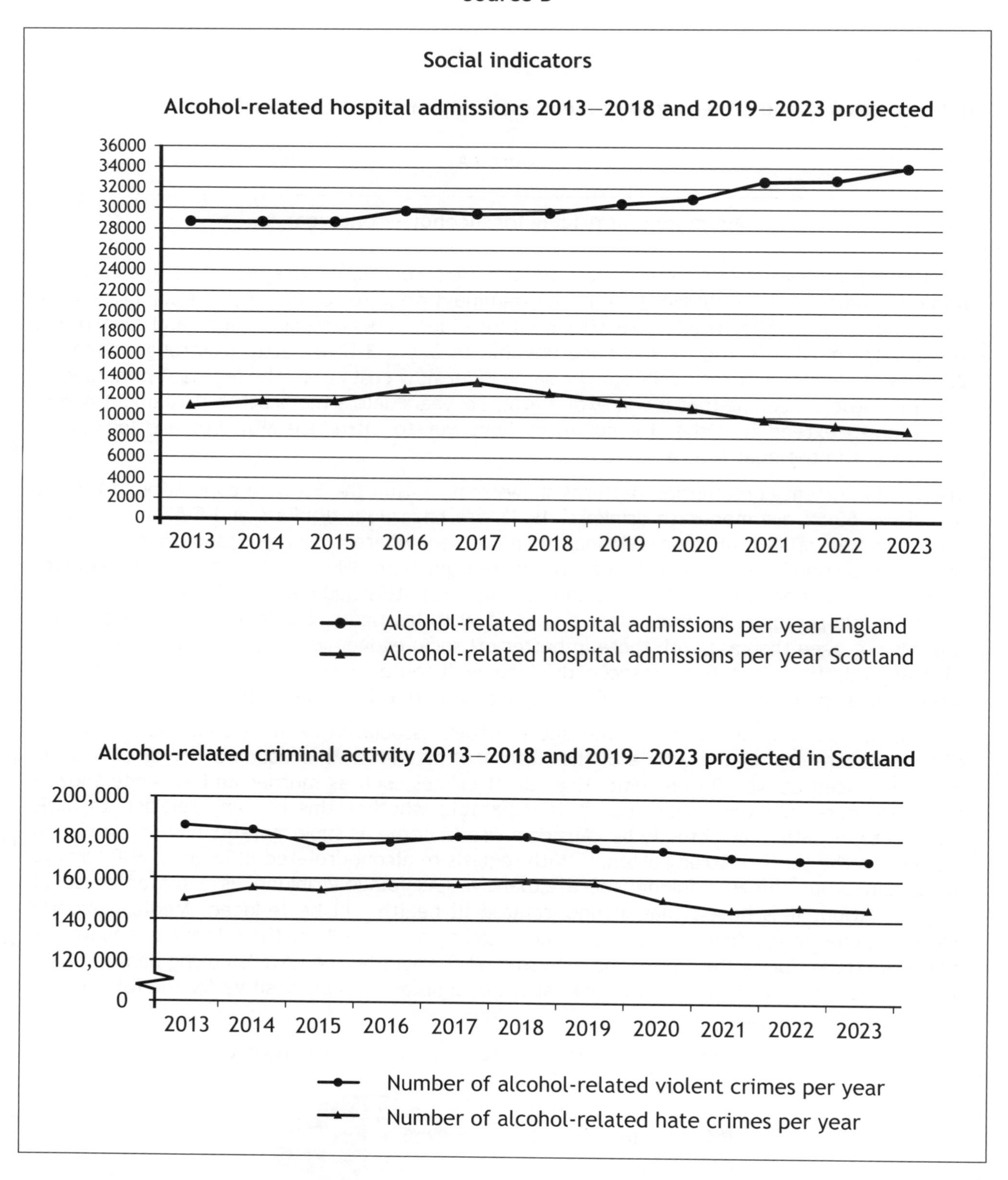

MARKS

Question 1 (continued)

Source C

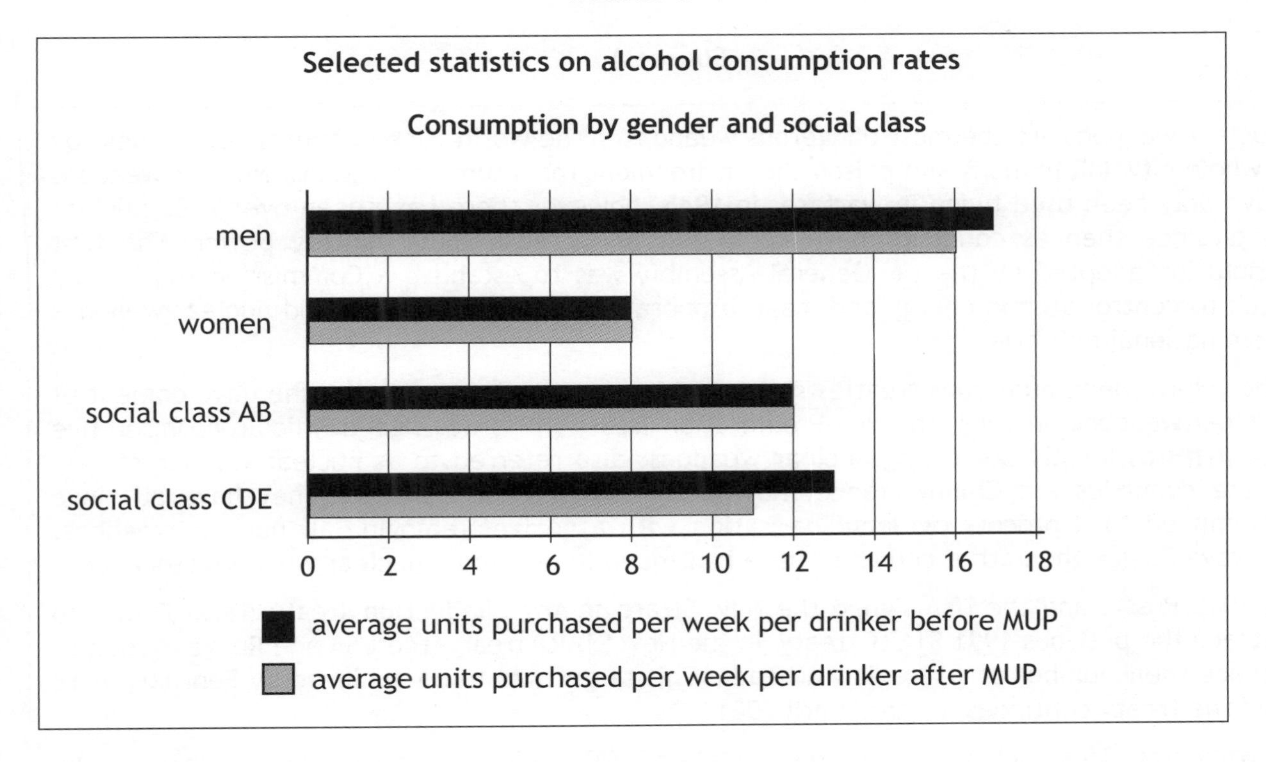

Attempt the following question, using only the information in Sources A, B and C on *Pages three*, *four* and above.

What conclusions can be drawn about minimum unit pricing for alcohol in Scotland?

You must draw conclusions about

- minimum unit pricing and consumption by socio-economic group
- minimum unit pricing and crime rates
- minimum unit pricing and health.

You must also make an overall conclusion on the **extent** to which people's drinking habits have changed due to minimum unit pricing. **10**

[Turn over

Question 2

Study Sources A and B then attempt the question that follows.

Source A

Nuclear weapons are the most dangerous weapons in the world. One missile is able to destroy a whole city, kill millions and poison the environment for future generations. Nuclear weapons have only been used twice in warfare, in 1945, however there have been over 2000 nuclear tests since then as countries have competed to increase their military power. The first resolution adopted by the UN General Assembly was to establish a Commission that would seek to control atomic energy and make proposals to eliminate atomic and nuclear weapons from national militaries.

There have been numerous treaties signed between countries to prevent the development of nuclear weapons. In 1968, the Non-Proliferation Treaty (NPT) was signed which recognised five countries as legally possessing nuclear weapons, also referred to as nuclear weapon states. These countries are China, France, Russia, the UK and the USA, and they have all since committed to a process of denuclearisation with a goal of removing all nuclear weapons. However, since then other countries have continued to develop a nuclear weapons stockpile.

In 2010 Russia and the USA signed the New Strategic Arms Reduction Treaty (New START) to replace the previous 1991 START treaty. In the New START treaty, the USA and Russia agreed to reduce their number of strategic warheads. This target was to be achieved by February 2018 and the treaty continues in force until 2021.

Further steps to a nuclear-free world were taken in 2017 with the approval of the treaty on the Prohibition of Nuclear Weapons by 122 countries. Those who have signed the treaty agree to pursue measures on disarmament and to make commitments against the use, development and stockpiling of nuclear weapons. The treaty was signed by the UN Secretary General in November 2017 and has been celebrated as a step towards a nuclear-free world. However, many argue that it will have no practical impact and it faces significant criticism from the five nuclear weapons states who have refused to attend the treaty negotiations.

Public opinion poll

	strongly agree	agree	don't know	disagree	strongly disagree
The threat of nuclear weapons has been reduced in recent years.	14	43	18	19	6
The world would be safer without nuclear weapons.	11	23	22	32	12

MARKS

Question 2 (continued)

Source B

Nuclear disarmament — an uncertain future?

Since Donald Trump became President of the United States tensions and uncertainty in international diplomacy have increased. In Donald Trump's first address to the UN General Assembly he threatened to *'totally destroy'* North Korea if they continue their testing of ballistic missiles. In 2017 North Korea launched 23 missiles in an effort to develop a long-range nuclear warhead. In early 2018 tensions further flared as Donald Trump tweeted that *'I too have a nuclear button, but it is a much bigger and more powerful one than his, and my button works!'* North Korea has now conducted six nuclear tests to prove their ability to fire nuclear weapons.

The process of nuclear disarmament has also faced setbacks in the Middle East where Donald Trump has withdrawn from Barack Obama's 2015 deal with Iran that would have seen UN weapons inspectors enter Iran to ensure that they are not developing nuclear weapons. Many fear that this will lead Iran's President Hassan Rouhani to resume aspects of their nuclear programme. Despite both the USA and Russia meeting their New START targets, the treaty remains controversial. Trump has called the New START treaty a *'bad deal'* which is *'one-sided.'* The treaty will expire in 2021 and so far there has been no initial discussion between the USA and Russia on what could replace it. Whilst some commentators are fearful that Trump will refuse to sign a new deal, others suggest that this is only *'bluster'* and that the advantages and successes of the New START deal so far will improve the likelihood of a renewal of the treaty.

Global nuclear warheads stockpile

Country	1965	1985	2017
Russia	6144	38582	4500
USA	31139	23368	4000
France	32	360	300
China	5	222	270
UK	271	350	214
Pakistan			140
India			130
Israel		42	80
North Korea			15
Total	**37591**	**62924**	**9649**

Attempt the following question, using only the information in Sources A and B on *Page six* and above.

To what extent is it accurate to state that efforts to reduce the threat posed by nuclear weapons have been successful? 10

[Turn over

Question 3

Study Sources A, B and C then attempt the question that follows.

Source A

Only a third of Scots support independence

Q. The second question will ask whether you agree or disagree with a proposal to extend the powers of the Scottish Parliament to enable Scotland to become an independent country, separate from the UK. If the referendum was held tomorrow, would you vote to agree or disagree with this proposal:

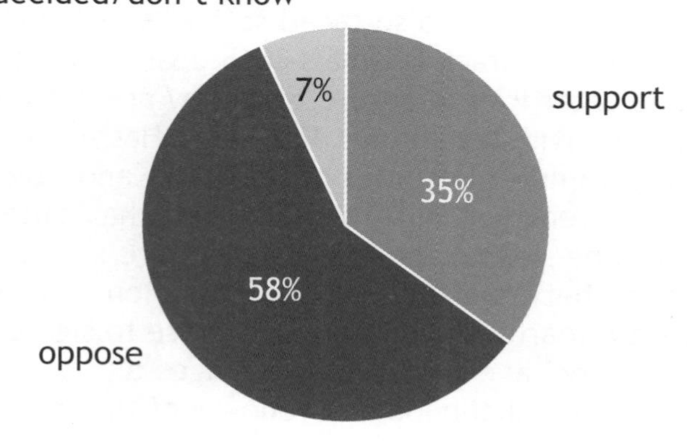

Sample size: 1,002 Scottish adults, 18+, 25th–29th August 2011

Source: Ipsos Mori 2011 (international polling company)

Source B

Source: Vote Leave, official campaign in favour of the UK leaving the European Union, 2016

MARKS

Question 3 (continued)

Source C

Source: The Green Party, 2017 election leaflet

Attempt the following question, using only the information in Sources A, B and C on *Page eight* and above.

To what extent are Sources A, B and C reliable?

You must provide an overall conclusion on the most reliable source of information. **8**

[END OF QUESTION PAPER]

[BLANK PAGE]

DO NOT WRITE ON THIS PAGE

HIGHER

Answers

ANSWERS FOR

SQA HIGHER MODERN STUDIES 2019

General Marking Principles for Higher Modern Studies (2018)

Marking principles for each question type

For each of the question types the following provides an overview of marking principles.

The types of questions used in this paper are:

- discuss ... [**20-mark** extended response]
- to what extent ... [**20-mark** extended response]
- evaluate ... [**12-mark** extended response]
- analyse ... [**12-mark** extended response]
- to what extent is it accurate to state that ... [information-handling question – **8 marks**]
- what conclusions can be drawn ... [information-handling question – **8 marks**]

Extended response (12 or 20 marks)

For 12-mark responses, up to a **maximum of 8 marks** will be awarded for knowledge and understanding (description, explanation and exemplification). The remaining marks will be awarded for the demonstration of higher-order skills of analysis **or** evaluation. Where a candidate makes more analytical/evaluative points than are required to gain the **maximum allocation of 4 marks**, these can be credited as knowledge and understanding marks provided they meet the criteria for this.

For 20-mark responses, up to **8 marks** will be awarded for knowledge and understanding (description, explanation and exemplification). The remaining marks will be awarded for the demonstration of higher-order skills of analysis **and** evaluation **and** structured argument. Where a candidate makes more analytical/evaluative points than are required to gain the maximum allocation of marks, these can be credited as knowledge and understanding marks provided they meet the criteria for this.

In the *Democracy in Scotland and the United Kingdom* and the *Social Issues in the United Kingdom* sections, candidates should be credited for responses which refer to Scotland only, to the United Kingdom only, or to both Scotland and the United Kingdom in their responses.

Analyse questions

- Candidates will identify parts of an issue, the relationship between these parts and their relationships with the whole; draw out and relate implications.

Evaluate questions

- Candidates will make a judgement based on criteria; determine the value of something.

Discuss questions

- Candidates will communicate ideas and information on the issue in the statement. Candidates will be credited for analysing and evaluating different views of the statement/viewpoint.

To what extent questions

- Candidates will analyse the issue in the question and come to a conclusion or conclusions which involve an evaluative judgement which is likely to be quantitative in nature.

Source-based questions that assess information-handling skills (8 marks)

- Questions will have at least two sources at an appropriate SCQF level.
- Award up to **3 marks** for a single developed point depending on the use of the evidence in the sources and the quality of the analysis/evaluation.
- Credit candidates who synthesise information both within and between sources.
- For full marks candidates must refer to all sources in their answer.

'Objectivity' questions

- For full marks candidates must make an overall judgement as to the extent of the accuracy of the given statement. **Maximum 6 marks** if no overall judgement is made on extent of accuracy of the statement.
- Credit may be given up to **2 marks** for answers which evaluate the usefulness or reliability of the source; however, this is not required for full marks.

'Conclusions' questions

- For full marks candidates must make conclusions/judgements based upon evidence relating to the specific prompts in the question.
- Candidates are also required to make an overall conclusion about the issue in the question.

Higher Modern Studies marking grid for 12-mark questions (KU = 8 marks; analysis/evaluation = 4 marks)

	1 mark	2 marks	3 marks	4 marks
Range of relevant knowledge Accurate, relevant, up to date.	One relevant aspect of the issue given with some description.	Two relevant aspects of the issue given with some description **or** one relevant aspect covered with detailed and accurate description.	One relevant aspect of the issue with detailed and accurate description **and** one relevant aspect with some description.	At least two relevant aspects with detailed and accurate descriptions – these should include the key aspects of the issue.
Quality of explanation/ exemplification of knowledge Up to a **maximum of 8 marks** available for knowledge and understanding.	Some explanation of one aspect of the issue **or** relevant exemplification.	Some explanation of two relevant aspects of the issue **or** detailed explanation of one aspect of the question which may include relevant exemplification.	Detailed explanation of one relevant aspect of the issue with relevant exemplification **and** some explanation of one aspect of the question.	At least two aspects of the question, fully explained, which relate closely to the key aspects of the question **and** extended, relevant, accurate and up-to-date exemplification.
Analysis/evaluation Comments that identify relationships/implications/make judgements. Up to **4 marks*** available.	One relevant and accurate analytical or evaluative comment.	One relevant and accurate analytical or evaluative comment that is justified **or** exemplified **or** two different relevant and accurate analytical/evaluative comments.	One developed relevant and accurate analytical or evaluative comment that is justified **and** exemplified – this should relate closely to a key aspect of the question.	One extended, accurate and justified analytical or evaluative comment of an insightful nature which relates closely to the key aspects of the question and is exemplified.

*Where a candidate makes more analytical/evaluative points than are required to gain the **maximum allocation of 4 marks**, these can be credited as knowledge and understanding marks provided they meet the criteria for this.

Answers to **12-mark** questions should demonstrate at least two relevant aspects of knowledge. For **full marks** in the KU aspect of the question **(8 marks)**, a response **must** include a range of points, have detailed explanation, and include accurate exemplification.

Maximum of 6 marks available **(from 8 for KU)** if there is no accurate or relevant exemplification.

For **full marks (12/12)**, a response **must** include a range of points, have detailed description/explanation, include a range of accurate exemplification and analysis or evaluation.

Higher Modern Studies marking grid for 20-mark questions (KU = 8 marks; analysis/evaluation = 12 marks)

	1 mark	2 marks	3 marks	4 marks	5–6 marks
Range of relevant knowledge Accurate, relevant, up to date.	One relevant aspect of the issue given with some description.	Two relevant aspects of the issue given with some description **or** one relevant aspect covered with detailed and accurate description.	One relevant aspect of the issue with detailed and accurate description **and** one relevant aspect with some description.	At least two relevant aspects with detailed and accurate descriptions – these should include the key aspects of the issue.	
Quality of explanation/ exemplification of the issue Up to a **maximum of 8 marks** available for knowledge and understanding.	Some explanation of one aspect of the issue **or** relevant exemplification.	Some explanation of two relevant aspects of the issue **or** detailed explanation of one aspect of the question which may include relevant exemplification.	Detailed explanation of one relevant aspect of the issue with relevant exemplification **and** some explanation of one aspect of the question.	At least two aspects of the question, fully explained, which relate closely to the key aspects of the question **and** extended, relevant, accurate and up-to-date exemplification.	
Analysis Comments that identify relationships/implications, explore different views or establish consequences/ implications. Up to **6 marks*** available.	One relevant and accurate analytical comment.	One relevant and accurate analytical comment that is justified **or** exemplified **or** two different relevant and accurate analytical comments.	One developed relevant and accurate analytical comment that is justified **and** exemplified; this should relate closely to a key aspect of the question.	One extended, accurate and justified analytical comment of an insightful nature which relates closely to the key aspects of the question **and** is exemplified.	At least two developed relevant and accurate analytical comments that are justified **and** exemplified. These should relate closely to the question and may be linked for **6 marks**.
Structure Structure which develops a consistent and clear line of argument. Up to **2 marks** available.	Clear structure that addresses the issue identified in the question.	Structure that clarifies the issue, presents evidence and develops a clear and consistent line or argument.			
Conclusions Evaluative comments which make a judgement(s) and or reach a conclusion(s) which address the key issues in the question. Up to **4 marks*** available.	One conclusion that addresses a key issue in the question.	One extended and balanced conclusion that addresses a key issue in the question **or** two conclusions that address key issues in the question.	One extended and balanced conclusion that is justified and directly addresses the key issue(s) in the question **or** two balanced conclusions that address the key issues in the question, one of which is extended.	One extended and balanced insightful conclusion that is justified and directly addresses the central aspects of the question **and** which considers a range of viewpoints.	

*Where a candidate makes more analytical/evaluative points than are required to gain the **maximum allocation of 4 marks**, these can be credited as knowledge and understanding marks provided they meet the criteria for this.

Answers to **20-mark** questions should demonstrate at least two relevant aspects of knowledge and provide detailed analysis and evaluation. For **full marks** in the KU aspect of the question (8/8), a response **must** include a range of points, have detailed explanation, and include a range of accurate exemplification.

Maximum of 6 marks available **(from 8 for KU)** if there is no exemplification.

For **full marks (20/20)**, a response **must** be structured, include a range of points, have detailed explanation, include a range of accurate and relevant exemplification and contain extended analysis and evaluation.

Higher Modern Studies marking grid for 8-mark source-based (objectivity/conclusions) questions

	1 mark	2 marks	3 marks	4 marks	5 marks	6 marks
Use of sources of evidence Up to **6 marks** available.	One relevant piece of evidence relating to one aspect of the issue is used from one source.	Two distinct pieces of evidence relating to one aspect of the issue are linked which may be from within a single source or between sources.	Two distinct pieces of evidence relating to one aspect of the issue are synthesised which may be from within a single source or between sources and an evaluative commentary is given.	In addition: a second aspect of the issue is addressed with reference to one relevant piece of evidence.	In addition: a second aspect of the issue is addressed with reference to linked evidence.	In addition: a second aspect of the issue is addressed with reference to synthesised evidence including an evaluative comment.
Objectivity Analysis of the accuracy/selectivity/objectivity of a given view against evidence is presented. Up to **2 marks** available.	An objective assessment of a given view is stated, based on evidence presented from the sources.	A detailed objective assessment of a given view is stated, based on evidence presented from the sources.	1. For **full marks** candidates **must** refer to all sources in their answer. A **maximum of 6 marks** if all sources are not used. 2. **Objectivity questions.** (i) Up to **6 marks** are available for the accurate evaluation of the given view using evidence. (ii) Candidates may also be credited up to **2 marks** on any comment/analysis of the origin and reliability of the sources. (iii) Up to **2 marks** are available for an overall judgement as to the extent of accuracy/objectivity of the view. 3. **Conclusions questions.** For **full marks** candidates **must** make evaluative comments/judgement(s)/draw a conclusion about each of the points given in the question. **2 further marks** are available for an overall summative conclusion.			
Conclusion Overall evaluative comment(s) derived from a judgement of the evidence presented. Up to **2 marks** available.	Overall conclusion is clear and supported by evidence from the sources.	Overall conclusion is insightful and supported by detailed evidence from the sources.				

HIGHER MODERN STUDIES 2018

Section 1 — Democracy in Scotland and the United Kingdom

Question		General Marking Instructions for this type of question	Max mark	Specific Marking Instructions for this question
1.	(a)	An analysis mark should be awarded where a candidate uses their knowledge and understanding/a source, to identify relevant components (eg of an idea, theory, argument, etc) and clearly show at least one of the following: • links between different components • links between component(s) and the whole • links between components(s) and related concepts • similarities and contradictions • consistency and inconsistency • different views/interpretations • possible consequences/ implications • the relative importance of components • understanding of underlying order or structure. Credit responses that make reference to: • advantages of leaving the EU • disadvantages of leaving the EU. Up to **8 marks** for KU (description, explanation and exemplification) and up to **4 marks** for analytical comments. Award up to **6 marks** per point. Candidates should be credited up to **full marks** if they answer within a Scottish context only, a UK context only or refer to both Scotland and the UK as appropriate. Where a candidate makes more evaluative points than are required to gain the maximum allocation of 4 marks, these can be credited as knowledge and understanding marks provided they meet the criteria for this.	12	*Candidates can be credited in a number of ways up to a **maximum of 12 marks**.* **Credit reference to aspects of the following:** **Potential impact of leaving the European Union (EU):** • sovereignty — EU laws, regulations and directives on issues such as farming and fisheries, environment, transport deals, energy etc • more control over immigration/border • security — increasing amount of terror attacks in Europe • free to negotiate trade (with EU and internationally) • save on the cost of membership — annual net contribution of £8 billion approx • global influence • economic benefits — trade, investment and jobs. The EU single market allows the free movement of goods, services, capital and workers • approximately half of all UK trade is conducted with the EU • free movement — varied benefits in relation to travel, study and employment. Over a million Britons live in other EU countries and millions more visit each year. Flights to Europe and using mobile phones on holiday are cheaper thanks to the EU. British tourists enjoy free or cheaper healthcare in other EU countries. Britain is not part of the Schengen area and retains some control over borders • employment rights — the EU has delivered guaranteed holiday pay, paid maternity leave, and increased protection in the workplace • security — safer as part of an EU that fights terrorism together. Europol membership allows EU wide sharing of intelligence and cross-border support. *Any other valid point that meets the criteria described in the general marking instructions for this kind of question.* **Possible approaches to answering this question:** **Response 1:** One potential impact of leaving the EU is that we would not need to pay a membership fee to be part of the union. It is estimated that this fee, after deducting rebates and returning money, comes to around £35 million per day **(2 marks KU)**. This means the UK government could choose to spend this money in other ways, on areas such as health and education **(1 mark analysis)**. **(Total 3 marks — 2 marks KU, 1 mark analysis).** **Response 2:** One potential impact of leaving the EU is that it could be harmful for the UK's security. The growth of cross-border crime and the threat of international terrorism linked to Islamic State all raise questions about how EU nations can work together to keep people safe **(1 mark KU)**. A benefit of EU membership is that member states share criminal intelligence with other member states and this works to combat potential threats **(1 mark KU)**. As a consequence of leaving the EU, Britain may lose access to this information-sharing network, meaning greater risk for UK citizens **(1 mark analysis)**. **(Total 3 marks — 2 marks KU, 1 mark analysis).**

Question		General Marking Instructions for this type of question	Max mark	Specific Marking Instructions for this question
1.	(a)	(continued)		**Response 3:** Within the EU there is free movement of people from and across European countries. Over a million British people live abroad in the EU and 15,000 UK students took part in the European Union's Erasmus student exchange scheme in 2017 **(2 marks KU).** This highlights that UK citizens rely on EU membership for straightforward travel and residency. Furthermore, the EU has enabled people to travel freely across national borders, boosting the economy. Millions of UK citizens have enjoyed cheap flights to European cities and many other EU nationalities have come to visit the UK, boosting our tourism industry in the process **(2 marks analysis).** **(Total 4 marks — 2 marks KU, 2 marks analysis).**
	(b)	An analysis mark should be awarded where a candidate uses their knowledge and understanding/a source, to identify relevant components (eg of an idea, theory, argument, etc) and clearly show at least one of the following: • links between different components • links between component(s) and the whole • links between components(s) and related concepts • similarities and contradictions • consistency and inconsistency • different views/interpretations • possible consequences/implications • the relative importance of components • understanding of underlying order or structure. Credit responses that make reference to: • newspaper • television • radio • social media/internet • discussion of relative importance of different factors within the media • social class • class dealignment • credit highly those candidates who integrate factors and highlight links between the media and social class. Up to **8 marks** for KU (description, explanation and exemplification) and up to **4 marks** for analytical comments. Award up to **6 marks** per point. Candidates should be credited up to **full marks** if they answer within a Scottish context only, a UK context only or refer to both Scotland and the UK as appropriate.	12	*Candidates can be credited in a number of ways up to a* ***maximum of 12 marks.*** **Credit reference to aspects of the following:** • analysis of the influence of the media on voting behaviour • analysis of the relative influence of different aspects of the media • analysis of the media's influence on other factors which can affect voting behaviour. **Do not credit:** • answers which consider other factors without linking them in any way to the influence of the media. **Newspapers:** • newspapers have a significant influence on the electorate, approximately 7 million newspapers are sold daily in the UK • newspapers have the power to influence the political agenda by shaping public opinion on current issues • newspapers are often politically biased and will openly support a specific party. This support becomes increasingly partisan around election time and on election day • newspapers will spin stories to suit a political agenda • reference to a variety of examples of newspapers backing political parties and party electoral success eg the Sun and the Conservatives in 2015, the Scottish Sun and the SNP in 2016, attacks on Jeremy Corbyn in 2017 • newspapers can break stories about politicians and parties as well as negatively influence public perception of politicians eg Ed Miliband when Labour leader • parties employ 'spin doctors' to manage the media, including newspaper coverage. **Television:** • television broadcasting in the UK has to adhere to strict impartiality rules when it comes to politics • television is the main source of news consumption for most UK citizens • televised leaders debates have now become a feature of UK general elections. The influence of these debates is questionable but they do allow for the public to scrutinise policy and leadership • the debates are discussed and dissected on social media platforms and evaluated the next day in newspapers • TV shows such as Peston on Sunday, Question Time and Daily Politics can give the electorate insight into political issues of the day. **Radio:** • prominent politicians such as Alex Salmond and Nigel Farage have weekly phone-in slots on digital radio stations • radio shows such as BBC Radio's Pienaar's Politics and Today show provide a source of news and political analysis for listeners.

Question		General Marking Instructions for this type of question	Max mark	Specific Marking Instructions for this question
1.	(b)	(continued) Where a candidate makes more evaluative points than are required to gain the maximum allocation of 4 marks, these can be credited as knowledge and understanding marks provided they meet the criteria for this.		**Social media/internet:** • increasing use of social media platforms such as Twitter and Facebook by the general public • increasing use of social media by politicians and political parties (2017) • political movements can begin on social media through hashtagging • social media more influential among younger voters (2017) • social media often referred to as an 'echo chamber' where political issues are discussed as opposed to a place where genuine political influence is exerted • social media users tend to only engage with people and politicians who mirror their own views • growing importance and rise of 'fake news' on social media platforms. *Any other valid point that meets the criteria described in the general marking instructions for this kind of question.* **Possible approaches to answering this question:** **Response 1:** Party Political Broadcasts (PPB) give parties a short slot or advert on TV to get across to the electorate their message and policies. This is a straightforward method of providing political information **(1 mark KU)**. However, how effective PPBs can be is questionable as people tend to find them unengaging and uninspiring **(1 mark analysis)**. **(Total 2 marks — 1 mark KU, 1 mark analysis).** **Response 2:** The influence of newspapers and social media is often debated. Older people, who are more likely to vote, will still get their political information from 'old media' such as newspapers and television **(1 mark KU)**. Younger people engage with politics online through platforms such as Twitter and Facebook **(1 mark KU)**. The fact the Conservatives spent £100,000 per month on Facebook political advertising indicates that they attach significant importance to 'new media'. This spend was significantly more than other parties and it helped them win the 2015 General Election **(2 marks analysis)**. **(Total 4 marks — 2 marks KU, 2 marks analysis).** **Response 3:** Newspapers are not obliged to be impartial during election time and will often back a certain political party. Millions of UK voters claim to read a newspaper on a daily basis. This means that the political news they read may have a 'spin' on it to portray a party in a certain way — almost all newspapers will have a political agenda behind their reporting. This is believed to heavily influence voters **(1 mark KU, 1 mark analysis).** In 2015, newspapers that backed the Conservatives had the largest amount of readers with the Sun having around 2 million daily readers and the Daily Mail having around 1.5 million **(1 mark KU)**. The Conservatives won the 2015 election, with this support highlighting the influence newspapers can have on the outcome **(1 mark analysis)**. However, newspaper circulation sales are declining and 'new media' is becoming more popular. With all the major political parties on Facebook and Twitter, they are gaining more direct public attention **(1 mark analysis)**. **(Total 5 marks — 2 marks KU, 3 marks analysis).**

Question		General Marking Instructions for this type of question	Max mark	Specific Marking Instructions for this question
2.		The candidate is required to interpret/evaluate up to three complex sources of information detecting and explaining the extent of objectivity. In order to achieve credit candidates must show evidence which supports the extent of accuracy in a given viewpoint: • award up to **3 marks** for appropriate use of evidence depending on the quality of the explanation and the synthesis of the evidence for any one explanation of the extent of objectivity • for **full marks** candidates must refer to all sources in their answer • for **full marks** candidates must make an overall judgement as to the extent of the accuracy of the given statement • **maximum of 6 marks** if no overall judgement made on extent of accuracy of the statement. Candidates may be awarded up to a **maximum of 2 marks** for incorporating an evaluation of the reliability of the sources in their explanations although this is not mandatory.	8	*Candidates can be credited in a number of ways up to a **maximum of 8 marks**.* **Evidence that supports the view** *('the Scottish Parliament's committees fulfil their roles effectively').* • Source A – committees play an important role in holding the SNP government to account because the Scottish Parliament is a single-chamber Parliament. • Source A – the membership of the committees is made up of MSPs from every party, with Committee Conveners, who chair meetings and set agendas, being drawn from different parties – impacting their ability to hold the government to account. • Source A – every piece of legislation that comes out of Holyrood comes under the scrutiny of one or more of the Scottish Parliament's committees. This has meant hundreds of amendments. • Source A – most committees allow the general public to attend which ensures transparency and scrutiny of the SNP government. This public scrutiny effectively holds government to account. • Source C – committees engage in short and 'snappy' inquiries with the potential to provide timely advice to government. They have the power to compel attendance. • Source A – states that the public think the PPC is a 'credit to our democracy'. • Source C – 64% think the Public Petition Committee system is effective/very effective. **Response 1:** Committees can hold the government to account as in Source A it states that 'every piece of legislation that comes out of Holyrood comes under the scrutiny of one or more of the Scottish Parliament's committees' **(1 mark, relevant source evidence).** **Response 2:** Committees are effective in holding inquiries. Source B shows an increasing number of inquiries held from 20 in 2012 to 30 in 2017. Not only are more being held but witnesses can be compelled to attend **(2 marks, evidence from two sources).** **Evidence that does not support the view** *('the Scottish Parliament's committees fulfil their roles effectively').* • Source A – a petition to scrap the Offensive Behaviour at Football Act received nearly 10,000 signatures, however the government wasn't forced to take action by this. • Source A – in Parliamentary Session 4 (2011–2016), 170 petitions were considered by the PPC. The equivalent committee in the Welsh Assembly considered 356 petitions in that time. • Source C – two thirds of those surveyed said that a second chamber would be more effective in carrying out the jobs of the committees. • Source B – only one piece of legislation from committees was passed in Parliamentary Session 4 (2011–2016), perhaps failing in one of its functions: to introduce legislation. • Source C – the dominance of the SNP means their MSPs make up a large proportion of membership in each committee. For example, on the Education and Skills Committee there are 11 members – 5 of which are SNP MSPs including the Committee's Convenor (links with Source B, SNP convene 8/16 committees) – perhaps reducing their effectiveness in holding government to account. • Source C – Scottish Parliamentary committees seem to be lacking the resources and time to conduct inquiries at the same rate as other comparable bodies, such as the Welsh Assembly. Source B shows that the Welsh Assembly consistently conducts more inquiries than the Scottish Parliament.

Question		General Marking Instructions for this type of question	Max mark	Specific Marking Instructions for this question
2.		(continued)		**Response 3:** Committees are not successful in holding the government to account in Scotland as Source C states that the dominance of the SNP means their MSPs make up a large proportion of membership in each committee. For example, on the Education and Skills Committee there are 11 members – 5 of which are SNP MSPs including the Committee's Convenor. This highlights that the SNP make up nearly 50% of membership. This links with Source B which tells us that the SNP also convene half of all committees (8/16). This makes it very difficult for the committee system to hold the SNP government to account as their MSPs can control committee work. **(3 marks, synthesised source use and evaluative comment)** **Response 4:** The Scottish Parliament's committees do not fulfil their roles effectively as they only conduct around 60% of the inquiries when compared to the Welsh Assembly (Source B). Also, there was only one piece of committee legislation passed. This does not compare favourably with just under the 70 pieces of Government legislation. Committees are clearly not effective in this role as the other three sources of legislation all managed to pass more laws (Source B) **(3 marks, synthesised source use and evaluative comment).** Candidates may also be credited up to **2 marks** on any comment/analysis of the origin and reliability of the source. • Source A is unreliable as it is adapted **(0 marks).** • Source A is unreliable as it is adapted. We have no idea how much of the article is original. We also have no idea who adapted the source or their motivation for doing so **(2 marks).** • Source B is reliable as the information has been taken from official government websites and the information will be reliable, verified and up to date and can therefore be considered trustworthy **(2 marks).** • Source C is unreliable as it is from a blog **(0 marks).** • Source C is unreliable as the blog will be influenced by the Professor's personal opinion **(1 mark).** • Source C includes survey data but no date is given. We have no idea when people were asked so the information may be old and out of date **(2 marks).** • Source C includes survey data but no sample information is given. We do not know if all age groups have been asked, if males and females are equally represented or how many in total were sampled **(2 marks).** • Source C is reliable as the Professor will be an educated person knowledgeable on the topic. However, this may be his/her personal opinion **(2 marks).** For **full marks**, candidates **must** make an overall judgement as to the extent of the accuracy of the given statement: • the statement is largely inaccurate as committees undoubtedly struggle to hold the Government to account in Scotland. They conduct fewer inquiries than other parliaments in the UK, consider fewer public petitions and the whole committee system is undermined by the dominance of the governing party who convene 8 out of the 16 committees **(2 marks).** • the statement is true to a certain extent **(0 marks).** • the statement is mainly untrue as committees fail to scrutinise the SNP Government due to committee membership issues **(1 mark).** • the statement is fairly accurate because committees are successful as they do hold the Government to account by looking at legislation **(1 mark).**

Question		General Marking Instructions for this type of question	Max mark	Specific Marking Instructions for this question
2.		(continued)		• overall, the statement is equally accurate and inaccurate. On the one hand committees can be successful as they scrutinise all legislation that becomes law, however committees are unsuccessful as they fail to hold as many inquiries as other parliaments **(2 marks)**. • the statement is true to a certain extent as although only one Committee Bill was passed, they have amended Government legislation hundreds of times **(1 mark)**.

Section 2 – Social Issues in the United Kingdom

Question		General Marking Instructions for this type of question	Max mark	Specific Marking Instructions for this question
3.	(a)	Evaluation involves making judgements based on criteria, drawing conclusions on the extent to which a view is supported by the evidence; counter-arguments including possible alternative interpretations; the overall impact/ significance of the factors when taken together; the relative importance of factors in relation to the context. Credit responses that make reference to: • the nature of social inequality • a socio-economic group and the impact of inequalities on it • an evaluation of the impact of inequality on an identified socio-economic group. Up to **8 marks** for KU (description, explanation and exemplification) and up to **4 marks** for analytical/ evaluative comment. Award up to **6 marks** per point. Candidates should be credited up to **full marks** if they answer within a Scottish context only, a UK context only or refer to both Scotland and the UK. Where a candidate makes more evaluative points than are required to gain the maximum allocation of 4 marks, these can be credited as knowledge and understanding marks provided they meet the criteria for this.	12	*Candidates can be credited in a number of ways up to a **maximum of 12 marks**.* **Credit reference to a group such as:** • age groups • gender • ethnicity • class • disability • the working poor. *Any other group that meets the criteria described in the general marking instructions for this kind of question. If a response considers more than one distinct group, it should only be credited for the one which attracts the highest mark.* **Possible approaches to answering this question:** **Response 1:** The pay gap between men and women continues to exist today and means that women earn approximately 15% less over their lifetime than men, creating an income inequality **(1 mark KU)**. **(Total 1 mark – 1 mark KU).** **Response 2:** The pay gap between men and women continues to exist today and means that women earn approximately 15% less over their lifetime than men, creating an income inequality **(1 mark KU)**. For example, it is estimated that women earn on average £330,000 less than men over the course of their working life **(1 mark KU)**. This can lead to women finding it more difficult to build up savings or a private pension and can create a significant inequality in later life **(1 mark evaluation)**. **(Total 3 marks – 2 marks KU, 1 mark evaluation).** **Response 3:** Despite equality legislation, women continue to face social inequality today. This is often due to family commitments and the fact that many women bear the responsibility of childcare which means that they are more likely to work in low paid, insecure work **(1 mark evaluation)**. For example, they are more likely to work in industries such as caring and administrative roles as opposed to men who are more likely to work in managerial work or in skilled trades **(1 mark KU)**. Traditional male occupations are often higher paid than traditional female occupations leading to a continued pay gap and income inequality **(1 mark evaluation)**. It is estimated that the pay gap has reached an average of 14.9% showing that income inequality continues to impact on women and makes them more vulnerable to low income and poverty **(1 mark KU)**. **(Total 4 marks – 2 marks KU, 2 marks evaluation).**

<table>
<tr><th colspan="2">Question</th><th>General Marking Instructions for this type of question</th><th>Max mark</th><th>Specific Marking Instructions for this question</th></tr>
<tr><td>3.</td><td>(a)</td><td>(continued)</td><td></td><td>Response 4:
Low paid workers are a group that is affected by social inequality as a result of rises in the cost of living. It is estimated that since the recession, food costs have risen by 26% and rent by 32% while for many, income rates have fallen or remained the same (2 marks KU). This means that low paid workers who often have only received the minimum wage do not earn enough to achieve a minimum living standard and experience significant social inequalities as a result (1 mark evaluation). The Poverty and Social Exclusion survey has estimated that around 18 million people in the UK cannot afford adequate housing conditions (1 mark KU). This shows that low pay can cause inequalities in housing and living standards which can go on to cause multiple deprivation meaning that low paid workers are a group that face significant social and economic inequalities (1 mark evaluation).
(Total 5 marks — 3 marks KU, 2 marks evaluation).</td></tr>
<tr><td></td><td>(b)</td><td>Evaluation involves making judgements based on criteria, drawing conclusions on the extent to which a view is supported by the evidence; counter-arguments including possible alternative interpretations; the overall impact/ significance of the factors when taken together; the relative importance of factors in relation to the context.
Credit responses that make reference to:
• sociological explanations of social inequality
• individualist explanations of social inequality.
Up to 8 marks for KU (description, explanation and exemplification) and up to 4 marks for evaluative comments.
Award up to 6 marks per point.
Candidates should be credited up to full marks if they answer within a Scottish context only, a UK context only or refer to both Scotland and the UK.
Where a candidate makes more evaluative points than are required to gain the maximum allocation of 4 marks, these can be credited as knowledge and understanding marks provided they meet the criteria for this.</td><td>12</td><td>Candidates can be credited in a number of ways up to a maximum of 12 marks.
Credit reference to aspects of the following:
• collectivist vs individualist approaches to tackling inequality
• theories about 'The Nanny State' and dependency culture — impact on individuals
• successes/failure of government actions which justify or reject collective approaches to welfare
• third sector approaches to tackling inequality such as food banks
• different approaches within the UK (for example the devolved administrations) and their relative financial costs
• differences between political parties in tackling social inequality.
Any other valid point that meets the criteria described in the general marking instructions for this kind of question.
Possible approaches to answering this question:
Response 1:
When the Welfare State was created after World War 2, one of its principal aims was to provide a safety net for the weakest in society and that government protection should extend from 'cradle to grave'. This is the view of collectivists who argue that the government is responsible for tackling social inequalities and that it has a responsibility to provide for the weakest in society (2 marks KU).
(Total 2 marks — 2 marks KU).
Response 2:
Parties such as the Conservatives argue that government should play a smaller role and that individuals should be responsible for tackling their own inequality (1 mark KU). They criticise the collectivist approach because it can create a dependency culture where people become reliant on the government for their income and do not seek out opportunities to provide for themselves (1 mark evaluation). Therefore, an individualist would convincingly argue that encouraging individual responsibility leads to a society where people take greater responsibility for their own lives showing that the government should not be fully responsible for tackling social inequality (1 mark evaluation).
(Total 3 marks — 1 mark KU, 2 marks evaluation).</td></tr>
</table>

Question		General Marking Instructions for this type of question	Max mark	Specific Marking Instructions for this question
3.	(b)	(continued)		**Response 3:** Collectivists believe that the government should be responsible for tackling social inequality by providing for people who are in poverty and face inequality. Collectivists argue that poverty is caused as a result of factors such as unemployment and low pay and that the government holds responsibility for helping reduce the impact of these factors **(2 marks KU)**. Unemployment can be caused by structural reasons such as the decline of manufacturing, times of recession or foreign competition **(1 mark KU)**. For example, the Tata steelworks in Port Talbot announced in 2016 that it would close, leading to job losses in the area **(1 mark KU)**. Collectivists argue that the government should be responsible for providing unemployment benefits to ensure that those who are affected do not fall into the poverty cycle as a result of the closure of the steelworks **(1 mark evaluation)**. **(Total 5 marks — 4 marks KU, 1 mark evaluation).** **Response 4:** Overall it is clear that social inequalities are a result of a growing poverty cycle in the UK where the most deprived communities face chronic unemployment and poor health **(1 mark evaluation)**. This leads to low social mobility which means that it is increasingly difficult for these groups to work their way out of poverty **(1 mark evaluation)**. As a result, the government must be held responsible for tackling these inequalities through the provision of universal healthcare and education, and through financial support to affected communities in the form of benefits and tax credits **(1 mark evaluation)**. By reducing the harmful effects of deprivation the government can ensure that inequality across the country is reduced and everybody is able to achieve a minimum living standard **(1 mark evaluation)**. **(Total 4 marks — 4 marks evaluation).**
	(c)	Evaluation involves making judgements based on criteria, drawing conclusions on the extent to which a view is supported by the evidence; counter-arguments including possible alternative interpretations; the overall impact/significance of the factors when taken together; the relative importance of factors in relation to the context. Credit responses that make reference to: • the ways in which crime has an economic impact • an evaluation of the economic impact of crime on society, individuals, government. Up to **8 marks** for KU (description, explanation and exemplification) and up to **4 marks** for analytical/evaluative comment. Award up to **6 marks** per point. Candidates should be credited up to **full marks** if they answer within a Scottish context only, a UK context only or refer to both Scotland and the UK.	12	*Candidates can be credited in a number of ways up to a **maximum of 12 marks**.* **Credit reference to aspects of the following:** • the economic impact of crime on individuals and families • the economic impact of crime on the local community • the economic impact on wider society. *Any other valid point that meets the criteria described in the general marking instructions for this kind of question.* **Possible approaches to answering this question:** **Response 1:** The majority of crimes (66%) are property crimes where people steal or damage another person's property **(1 mark KU)**. **(Total 1 mark — 1 mark KU).** **Response 2:** Property crime has a significant economic impact on the victims of that crime as the victims will lose the value of the property stolen. In some cases this might be a fairly small financial impact, for example in the case of street robberies the value of the property stolen may be fairly low **(1 mark evaluation)**. However, some property crimes have also led to a significant financial loss, for example in 2015 a gang of burglars raided a bank in Hatton Garden and stole £14million worth of jewellery. Most of this financial loss fell on the individual owners of the jewellery **(1 mark KU, 1 mark evaluation)**. **(Total 3 marks — 1 mark KU, 2 marks evaluation).**

<table>
<tr><th colspan="2">Question</th><th>General Marking Instructions for this type of question</th><th>Max mark</th><th>Specific Marking Instructions for this question</th></tr>
<tr><td>3.</td><td>(c)</td><td>(continued)

Where a candidate makes more evaluative points than are required to gain the maximum allocation of 4 marks, these can be credited as knowledge and understanding marks provided they meet the criteria for this.</td><td></td><td>Response 3:
Crime has a significant impact on wider society as the police, the court system and the various sentencing options all carry a high cost (1 mark evaluation). The Office for National Statistics estimate that in 2012 murder cost the economy £1.3 billion while theft cost society almost £4 billion (1 mark KU). The cost of crime can be particularly high when there are peaks in crimes, for example the London Riots proved to be very costly for society as riot police had to be moved to London from all over the country to deal with it, and the peak in offenders led to the court and prison system becoming overwhelmed (1 mark KU, 1 mark evaluation).

(Total 4 marks — 2 marks KU, 2 marks evaluation).

Response 4:
In areas where there are high crime rates the whole community can find itself economically impacted by crime. High crime rates can lead to the value of house prices in a community dropping and also increase house and car insurance premiums (1 mark evaluation). This affects those living in the area, but can also lead to them having less money to spend in shops in the area which may lead them to close. This could lead to higher unemployment in the area, and create a socially excluded community which can have greater costs on services such as the NHS and the benefit system which adds to the costs of crime to the country (2 marks evaluation). For example, Glasgow has a reputation for violent crime and also has a higher rate of alcoholism, drug addiction and unemployment which all brings significant costs to the government eg alcohol related crime costs Scotland £727 million (2 marks KU).

(Total 5 marks — 2 marks KU, 3 marks evaluation).</td></tr>
<tr><td></td><td>(d)</td><td>Evaluation involves making judgements based on criteria, drawing conclusions on the extent to which a view is supported by the evidence; counter-arguments including possible alternative interpretations; the overall impact/ significance of the factors when taken together; the relative importance of factors in relation to the context.

Credit responses that make reference to:
• sociological causes of crime
• an evaluation of the importance of society as a cause of crime.

Up to 8 marks for KU (description, explanation and exemplification) and up to 4 marks for evaluative comments.

Award up to 6 marks per point.

Candidates should be credited up to full marks if they answer within a Scottish context only, a UK context only or refer to both Scotland and the UK.</td><td>12</td><td>Candidates can be credited in a number of ways up to a maximum of 12 marks.

Credit reference to aspects of the following:
• Robert Merton/Strain theory of crime
• marxist theory
• functionalist theory
• social breakdown theory, anomie
• factors other than inequality which may cause crime
• reference to links between factors.

Any other valid point that meets the criteria described in the general marking instructions for this kind of question.

Possible approaches to answering this question:

Response 1:
Many people commit crime due to poverty and they commit crimes out of desperation. Those living in extreme poverty may turn to crimes, such as drug dealing, to boost their income.

(Total 1 mark — 1 mark KU).

Response 2:
Many people commit crime due to poverty and they commit crimes out of desperation. Extreme poverty can lead to opportunistic crimes like shoplifting or muggings (1 mark KU). However, it is also true that most people in poverty do not resort to crime, and therefore it is not completely true to say that poverty, and therefore inequality, causes crime (1 mark evaluation).

(Total 2 marks —1 mark KU, 1 mark evaluation).</td></tr>
</table>

<table>
<tr><th colspan="2">Question</th><th>General Marking Instructions for this type of question</th><th>Max mark</th><th>Specific Marking Instructions for this question</th></tr>
<tr><td>3.</td><td>(d)</td><td>(continued)

Where a candidate makes more evaluative points than are required to gain the maximum allocation of 4 marks, these can be credited as knowledge and understanding marks provided they meet the criteria for this.</td><td></td><td>Response 3:
People affected by poverty and unemployment can become socially isolated and excluded. Where there are communities of high social exclusion it could be argued that a condition of social breakdown begins to happen (1 mark KU). The theory of social breakdown argues that deprived communities experience greater levels of strain, frustration and disorganisation that make people more likely to commit crime (1 mark KU). A consequence of people not able to achieve success in life through legitimate means is that they may commit crimes that help them to achieve a better status (1 mark evaluation). People living in this type of community may join a gang and take part in gang-related crimes such as violence and drug dealing in order to improve their own status. This is also much more likely when society labels these areas and individuals as being involved with criminal activity (1 mark KU, 1 mark evaluation).

(Total 5 marks — 3 marks KU, 2 marks evaluation).

Response 4:
Marxist theory argues that crime is caused by the ruling classes who use the law as a means of social control (1 mark KU). Laws are used to encourage conformity among the masses, and also to control the working classes by focusing on crimes more likely to be committed by this group such as burglary and street crime (1 mark KU). This also leads to heavier policing in working class areas and consequently crime appears higher in these areas as people are more likely to be caught (1 mark evaluation). Marxists also argue that white collar crimes are ignored by the authorities, allowing for the ruling elite to maintain their power in the country (1 mark KU). This theory shows that government effectively criminalises the masses and therefore creates crime through attempting to control and imprison those who do not conform (1 mark evaluation).

(Total 5 marks — 3 marks KU, 2 marks evaluation).</td></tr>
<tr><td>4.</td><td></td><td>The candidate is required to interpret/evaluate up to three complex sources in order to reach conclusions.

In order to achieve credit candidates must show evidence which explains the conclusions reached:
• award up to 3 marks for appropriate use of evidence depending on the quality of the explanation and the synthesis of the evidence to reach any one conclusion
• for full marks candidates must refer to all sources in their answer
• for full marks candidates must reach conclusions about each of the points given and make and overall conclusion on the issue.</td><td>8</td><td>Candidates can be credited in a number of ways up to a maximum of 8 marks.

Possible approaches to answering this question:

Overcrowding and the living conditions of prisoners:

Response 1:
Overcrowding in prisons has led to the living conditions of prisoners being significantly reduced. Source A shows that prisoners are increasingly being kept in their cells for 23 hours during the day which is argued to be 'degrading'. Furthermore, overcrowded conditions in prisons such as Cornton Vale means that some prisoners have been denied sufficient access to toilets during the night (2 marks — synthesis of evidence from Source A with conclusion).

Response 2:
As a result of overcrowded conditions prisons are not able to provide accommodation that provides them with adequate healthcare. Human rights groups have criticised the practice of keeping prisoners in a cell for 23 hours a day as it can impact on their mental health (Source A) leading to a 60% increase in incidents of self-harm across prisons in England and Wales from around 20,000 in 2004 to 32,000 in 2014 (Source C). This shows that overcrowding has caused a significant deterioration in living conditions in prisons which contribute to poor mental health across the prison population (3 marks — synthesis of evidence from Source A and C with conclusion and evaluative comment).</td></tr>
</table>

Question		General Marking Instructions for this type of question	Max mark	Specific Marking Instructions for this question
4.		(continued)		**Response 3:** The overcrowded conditions in prisons have led to living conditions that breach prisoner rights. Frances Cook, the Chief Executive of the Howard League for Penal Reform, has said that 'prisons are increasingly providing restricted regimes, under which prisoners are locked in their cells for up to 23 hours a day' which is a degrading practice and impacts their mental health (Source A). This is supported by Source C which shows that self-harm has increased across prisons in England and Wales to 32,000 in 2014. Furthermore, prisoners in Scotland's only women's prison (Cornton Vale) have in the recent past been 'forced to use their sinks as toilets' during the night which inspectors described as a 'significant breach of human dignity' **(3 marks — synthesis of 3 pieces of evidence and conclusion).** **Overcrowding and safety in prisons:** **Response 4:** Overcrowded conditions in prisons have led to an increase of violence in prisons. The number of serious assaults inside prisons in England and Wales has increased significantly from around 1,250 in 2012 to just under 3,000 in 2015 (Source C). Furthermore, Source A shows that there has been a 'growing level of violence and rioting in prisons' and that the riot service was called out 203 times in 2013 which was an increase from 129 times in 2012 **(2 marks — synthesis of evidence from Source A and C and conclusion).** **Response 5:** Overcrowding in prisons has impacted on the ability of staff to keep the prison safe. Source A shows that Thameside prison has faced a 'rising level of gang violence' within the prison and that staff have struggled to deal with this. Thameside prison is overcrowded as shown in Source B as it currently holds 1,223 prisoners which is more than its CNA capacity of 932. This shows that overcrowding is a factor that causes increasing violence and reduces the safety of prisoners **(2 marks — synthesis of evidence and conclusion).** **Response 6:** Serious assaults and violence in prisons have been increasing in recent years, with nearly 3,000 serious assaults recorded in prisons in England and Wales in 2015 (Source C). This is due to overcrowding in prisons as staff are unable to control the large prison population (Source A). This is demonstrated by the fact that the number of riots in prisons has increased with the riot squad called out 203 times in 2013 which was an increase from 129 in 2012. I can conclude that overcrowded conditions reduce the safety of prisoners **(3 marks — synthesis of 3 pieces of evidence and conclusion).** **Overall conclusion:** **Response 7:** Overcrowding in prisons has increased in recent years **(0 marks — overall conclusion without supporting evidence).** **Response 8:** Overcrowding in prisons has increased in recent years and there are now 84,069 prisoners in England and Wales which is much higher than the 74,703 CNA capacity **(1 mark — overall conclusion with supporting evidence).** **Response 9:** Overall I can conclude that overcrowding in British prisons (Source A) has increased reaching a record high and the Prison Service is struggling to deal with the number of prisoners they have. Source B shows that they are currently holding 84,069 prisoners in England and Wales which is much higher than the 74,703 that is their CNA capacity **(2 marks — overall conclusion that is detailed and evaluative and is supported by evidence).**

Question		General Marking Instructions for this type of question	Max mark	Specific Marking Instructions for this question
4.		(continued)		**Response 10:** Overall, I can conclude that overcrowding is getting worse with four of the five prisons in Source B being beyond capacity and has doubled in the last twenty years (Source A). This has led to the biggest section of the public (39%) believing that more prisons should be built in order to tackle overcrowding (Source B). **(2 marks — overall conclusion supported by evidence).** **Response 11:** British prisons are facing a crisis as a result of overcrowding and a population which is much higher than its capacity. The current prison population is nearly 'double that of twenty years ago.' (Source A), and in England and Wales prisons are now holding 84,069 prisoners which is much higher than the 74,703 that is their CNA capacity (Source B) **(2 marks — overall conclusion supported by evidence).**

Section 3 — International Issues

Question		General Marking Instructions for this type of question	Max mark	Specific Marking Instructions for this question
5.	(a)	An analysis mark should be awarded where a candidate uses their knowledge and understanding/a source to identify relevant components (eg of an idea, theory, argument, etc) and clearly show at least one of the following: • links between different components • links between component(s) and the whole • links between components(s) and related concepts • similarities and contradictions • consistency and inconsistency • different views/interpretations • possible consequences/ implications • the relative importance of components • understanding of underlying order or structure. Evaluation involves making judgements based on criteria, drawing conclusions on the extent to which a view is supported by the evidence; counter-arguments including possible alternative interpretations; the overall impact/ significance of the factors when taken together; the relative importance of factors in relation to the context.	20	*Candidates can be credited in a number of ways up to a **maximum of 20 marks**.* **World Power: USA** **Credit reference to aspects of the following:** • income inequality — inequality has been growing markedly in the last 30 years, the top 1% have more than doubled their share of GDP. 40% of Americans live in poverty • ethnic inequality — Blacks and Hispanics are more likely to be poor experiencing greater levels of poverty than Whites or Asian Americans • educational inequality — dropout rates for Blacks and Hispanics of 20% and 30% compare poorly against the 11% and 3% for Whites and Asians • health inequality — 20% of Blacks have no health insurance compared to 10% of Whites. A third of Hispanics do not have health insurance • crime inequality — Blacks and Hispanics represented disproportionately in prison numbers • immigration — the broad range of social and economic inequalities experienced by both legal and illegal immigrants eg incomes, housing, crime, health etc. *Any other valid point that meets the criteria described in the general marking instructions for this kind of question.* **Possible approaches to answering this question:** **Response 1:** The United States of America is an extremely unequal society in which inequality exists across many social and economic indicators. In the last 30 years, inequality between groups in the US has grown markedly **(1 mark evaluation).** The richest 10% of Americans now average nearly nine times as much income as the poorest 90% **(1 mark KU).** **(Total 2 marks — 1 mark KU, 1 mark evaluation).**

Question		General Marking Instructions for this type of question	Max mark	Specific Marking Instructions for this question
5.	(a)	(continued) Credit responses that make reference to: • the nature of social and economic inequalities • the extent of social and economic inequalities • analysis and balanced comment of the extent of social and economic inequalities • provide a clear, coherent line of argument. Up to **8 marks** for KU (description, explanation and exemplification) and up to **12 marks** for analytical/evaluative comments. Award up to **6 marks** per point. Candidate may make reference to any member of the G20 group of countries, excluding the United Kingdom. Where a candidate makes more analytical/evaluative points than are required to gain the maximum allocation of 4 marks, these can be credited as knowledge and understanding marks provided they meet the criteria for this.		**Response 2:** Inequality exists in areas such as health, housing and education. Inequalities usually have an ethnic element with some ethnic groups such as Blacks and Hispanics more likely to experience inequality across these areas than Whites or Asian Americans **(1 mark analysis)**. This seems to be the case across many indicators – Blacks and Hispanics tend to do worse and suffer greater inequalities than Whites and Asian Americans **(1 mark evaluation)**. For example, 25% of Blacks and 23% of Hispanics are in poverty compared to 12% of Asian Americans and 9% of Whites **(1 mark KU)**. **(Total 3 marks – 1 mark KU, 1 mark analysis, 1 mark evaluation).** **Response 3:** Inequality exists across a great many areas in the United States. It is a land of growing inequality with an increasing number of millionaires and billionaires but also a growing number of those experiencing poverty and inequality. 40% of Americans live in poverty with 13 million children living in families that are officially classed as being in poverty. This is an increase of 2.5 million children since 2000 **(2 marks KU)**. Many of these Americans now living in poverty are unskilled Black workers who used to work in construction, manufacturing and car factories. These industries have gone and been replaced by high tech computing and service industry jobs. Blacks have been disproportionately affected by the global recession of 2008 with unemployment rates growing much more quickly for Blacks and Hispanics. This shows that certain ethnic groups are consistently disadvantaged in all aspects of American society **(2 marks KU, 1 mark evaluation)**. However, this is not completely true as there has been an increase and growth in the number of Blacks who would label themselves as middle class due to their educational and career status **(1 mark analysis)**. **(Total 6 marks – 4 marks KU, 1 mark analysis, 1 mark evaluation).** **World Power: South Africa** **Credit reference to aspects of the following:** • income inequality – 60% earn R42,000 per year ($7000) whereas 2% earn in excess of R360,000 ($50,000) • ethnic inequality – 90% of those in poverty are Black despite attempts by ANC to close poverty gap • educational inequality – 96% of Whites pass High School exams compared to 36% for Blacks • health inequality – differences between groups in terms of infant mortality – 65 per 1000 births for Blacks, 8 per 1000 for Whites • crime inequality – crime is a significant issue in South Africa with 59 murders per day, almost all of the victims are Black • immigration – the broad range of social and economic inequalities experienced by both legal and illegal immigrants eg incomes, housing, crime, health etc. *Any other valid point that meets the criteria described in the general marking instructions for this kind of question.* **Possible approaches to answering this question:** **Response 1:** The Republic of South Africa is a very unequal society with inequalities between groups prevalent across many social and economic areas **(1 mark evaluation)**. Inequality exists between ethnic groups with Blacks much more likely to be poorer than Whites in terms of poverty, education and other socio-economic indicators. 90% of those in poverty are Black **(1 mark KU)**. **(Total 2 marks – 1 mark KU, 1 mark evaluation).**

Question		General Marking Instructions for this type of question	Max mark	Specific Marking Instructions for this question
5.	(a)	(continued)		**Response 2:** South Africa is a deeply unequal society with differences between and within groups. According to the Gini co-efficient, South Africa is one of the most unequal countries in the world. The Theil Index which measures inequality between and within groups also indicates that inequality in South Africa is growing **(1 mark KU, 1 mark analysis).** Despite this inequality, there is a Black middle class which has increased in size from 300,000 in 1995 to over 3 million today. This demonstrates that, despite inequality, many South African Blacks are able to become more affluent and prosperous **(1 mark KU, 1 mark analysis).** **(Total 4 marks — 2 marks KU, 2 marks analysis).** **Response 3:** South Africa is a deeply unequal society with differences between and within groups. According to the Gini co-efficient, South Africa is one of the most unequal countries in the world. The Theil Index which measures inequality between and within groups also indicates that inequality in South Africa is growing **(1 mark KU, 1 mark analysis).** Despite this inequality, there is a Black middle class which has increased in size from 300,000 in 1995 to over 3 million today. This demonstrates that, despite inequality, many South African Blacks are able to become more affluent and prosperous **(1 mark KU, 1 mark analysis).** This rise can be explained by policies such as BEE. However, critics such as Archbishop Desmond Tutu argue that all BEE has done is create a Black elite while many Black South Africans live in 'de-humanising poverty' and many qualified Whites leave their own country as they are overlooked for jobs there. Demonstrating again that despite improvement for some, inequalities exist for others in South Africa **(2 marks evaluation).** **(Total 6 marks — 2 marks KU, 2 marks analysis, 2 marks evaluation).**
	(b)	An analysis mark should be awarded where a candidate uses their knowledge and understanding/a source, to identify relevant components (eg of an idea, theory, argument, etc) and clearly show at least one of the following: • links between different components • links between component(s) and the whole • links between components(s) and related concepts • similarities and contradictions • consistency and inconsistency • different views/interpretations • possible consequences/ implications • the relative importance of components • understanding of underlying order or structure. Evaluation involves making judgements based on criteria, drawing conclusions on the extent to which a view is supported by the evidence; counter-arguments including possible alternative interpretations; the overall impact/ significance of the factors when taken together; the relative importance of factors in relation to the context.	20	*Candidates can be credited in a number of ways up to a* ***maximum of 20 marks.*** **Credit reference to aspects of the following:** **World Power: USA** **People can influence government decision making in the following ways:** • by voting in County, State and Federal Elections for positions such as local Judge, dog catcher, Sheriff, Governor, Senator and President among others • political rights of US citizens enshrined in the US Constitution • citizens can also stand for elections themselves and are free to join political parties and campaign for candidates and policies • opportunities for people to participate in interest groups such as NRA, Black Lives Matter, Anonymous Movement and Occupy movement. Around 75% of Americans belong to at least one interest group • growth of Slacktivism • use of propositions within states to decide local laws such as Colorado's legalisation of marijuana • growing use of social media for political activity – Breitbart, 4Chan, AltRight. **Limits to influencing government decision making:** • obstacles to voter registration eg felony disenfranchisement • US political system overrepresents affluent white males and underrepresents women, ethnic minorities and the poor in the political process • differences in participation and registration rates between social classes and ethnic groups

Question		General Marking Instructions for this type of question	Max mark	Specific Marking Instructions for this question
5.	(b)	(continued) Credit responses that make reference to: • the political system of the world power • the opportunities that exist to influence decision making • the limits to these opportunities • analysis and balanced comment of the extent of influence • provide a clear, coherent line of argument. Up to **8 marks** for KU (description, explanation and exemplification) and up to **12 marks** for analytical/ evaluative comments. Award up to **6 marks** per point. Candidate may make reference to any member of the G20 group of countries, excluding the United Kingdom. Where a candidate makes more analytical/evaluative points than are required to gain the maximum allocation of 4 marks, these can be credited as knowledge and understanding marks provided they meet the criteria for this.		• interest group influence limited by lack of financial backing • cost of running and standing as a candidate financially prohibitive and limits involvement to only the very rich • criticisms that elected US politicians are lobbyists for American business interests rather than fully representing the will of their electorate • no legal right to join a trade union. TU membership showing steady decline. *Any other valid point that meets the criteria described in the general marking instructions for this kind of question.* **Possible approaches to answering this question:** **Response 1:** American citizens have rights and freedoms eg the right to assembly which means that they have the right to peacefully protest against the Government or an issue, such as the Anti Donald Trump rallies organised by American women after the inauguration of Donald Trump in 2017 **(2 marks KU).** **(Total 2 marks — 2 marks KU).** **Response 2:** One way in which American citizens can seek to influence the government is by running as a candidate for one of the many positions that are available on a County, State wide or National level **(1 mark KU).** However, standing for a national position such as Governor or President would need a lot of money to run a campaign which might put many people off from standing eg Obama campaign spent $985 million in getting him elected in 2012 **(1 mark KU, 1 mark analysis).** Therefore, it is difficult to put yourself forward for election if you are poor due to the cost. This shows that sometimes political participation in the USA is often easier if you are wealthy **(1 mark evaluation).** **(Total 4 marks — 2 marks KU, 1 mark analysis, 1 mark evaluation).** **Response 3:** American citizens can seek to have influence by joining a trade union or interest group. This would allow them to fight and campaign for things that they would like to see changes to **(1 mark KU).** Some types of political participation are more influential than others. For example, there are many different types of interest groups that campaign for different issues **(1 mark analysis).** Some of the most popular interest groups include the National Rifle Association (NRA) or Black Lives Matter **(1 mark KU).** In the USA, interest groups with the biggest memberships and budgets tend to have the most influence on government decision making eg the NRA **(1 mark evaluation).** However, participation rates for trade unions are much lower. There is no legal right to join a trade union in the USA and numbers of members are falling **(1 mark analysis).** There is now around 10% of public sector workers and 5% of private sector workers who are members of trade unions, compared to around 20% in 1983 **(1 mark KU).** **(Total 6 marks — 3 marks KU, 2 marks analysis, 1 mark evaluation).** **Credit reference to aspects of the following:** **World Power: China** **People can influence government decision making in the following ways:** • each level of government (local, district, regional and national) has elected officials with decision making powers • several other parties exist other than the CPC eg the China Democracy League has over 200,000 members • Chinese people can join a political party — around 7% of Chinese population (85 million) are members of the CPC • Chinese people do have access to the internet and can use social media sites such as Weibo

Question		General Marking Instructions for this type of question	Max mark	Specific Marking Instructions for this question
5.	(b)	(continued)		• there are numerous TV and radio stations • street protests are common eg growth of pro-Democracy movement in Hong Kong • growing membership of All-China Federation of Trade Unions and All Women Federation. **Limits to influencing government decision making:** • other parties only exist with the permission of the CPC and cannot act as opposition • all local elections are dominated by CPC and all candidates must be approved by them • CPC membership is not open to everyone and is by invite only • massive expenditure on internet monitoring, many western sites such as Google and the BBC are blocked • protests have to be sanctioned by the CPC and any dissent shown is ruthlessly dealt with by security forces • the media is heavily censored – China ranked 173 out of 178 countries on Index of Press Freedom. *Any other valid point that meets the criteria described in the general marking instructions for this kind of question.* **Possible approaches to answering this question:** **Response 1:** The Chinese state is essentially a one party dictatorship and as such, very few opportunities exist for citizens to influence the government. Elections do take place but all the candidates have to be vetted and agreed by the Chinese Communist Party before they are allowed to stand. **(Total 2 marks – 1 mark KU, 1 mark analysis).** **Response 2:** Chinese citizens can't access many western web pages and even searching using terms like 'democracy' or 'protest' are banned and blocked by what is referred to as the 'Great Firewall of China' **(1 mark KU).** This demonstrates the lengths that the Chinese government will go to in order to monitor and control any dissent or protest by ordinary Chinese citizens. However, these controls haven't stopped prodemocracy activists, particularly in Hong Kong, from protesting in favour of human rights issues and greater democracy. This highlights that despite controls being put in place, many Chinese people are risking arrest and imprisonment in order to campaign for more rights **(2 marks analysis, 1 mark evaluation).** **(Total 4 marks – 1 mark KU, 2 marks analysis, 1 mark evaluation).**
	(c)	An analysis mark should be awarded where a candidate uses their knowledge and understanding/a source, to identify relevant components (eg of an idea, theory, argument, etc) and clearly show at least one of the following: • links between different components • links between component(s) and the whole • links between components(s) and related concepts • similarities and contradictions • consistency and inconsistency • different views/interpretations • possible consequences/ implications • the relative importance of components	20	*Candidates can be credited in a number of ways up to a* ***maximum of 12 marks.*** **Credit reference to aspects of the following:** **World Issue: Development in Africa** Accept references to economic, political and social factors affecting development. **Economic factors:** • the effects of debt on development. Africa has a debt burden in excess of \$200 billion with annual debt repayments of \$14 billion which means money being diverted away to service World Bank and IMF debts • conditions attached by the IMF when lending to the region are punitive • use of cash crops to repay debt means farmers/countries can suffer due to market fluctuations and over supply • Africa's share of world trade has shrunk from 8% to around 2% during the last 30 years, affecting economic growth.

Question		General Marking Instructions for this type of question	Max mark	Specific Marking Instructions for this question
5.	(c)	(continued) • understanding of underlying order or structure. Evaluation involves making judgements based on criteria, drawing conclusions on the extent to which a view is supported by the evidence; counter-arguments including possible alternative interpretations; the overall impact/ significance of the factors when taken together; the relative importance of factors in relation to the context. Credit responses that make reference to: • factors which affect or influence a specific issue • the relative importance of these factors • analysis and balanced comment of specific factors on a giving issue • provide a clear, coherent line of argument. Up to **8 marks** for KU (description, explanation and exemplification) and up to **12 marks** for analytical/ evaluative comments. Award up to **6 marks** per point. Candidates may make reference to any world issues the impact of which extends beyond the boundaries of any single country. This impact may be regional or global in scale. Where a candidate makes more analytical/evaluative points than are required to gain the maximum allocation of 4 marks, these can be credited as knowledge and understanding marks provided they meet the criteria for this.		**Political factors:** • armed conflict affects crop cultivation, supply routes, cash being diverted away to finance the conflict • Oxfam reported that the financial impact of armed conflict in Africa over a 15-year period was nearly $300 billion, leading to, on average, 50% more infant deaths, a 5-year reduction in life expectancy and an increase in adult illiteracy • armed conflict creates refugees who are without food, water, shelter or medical aid • emergency aid often halted or disrupted due to armed conflict, and food production can often plummet • bad governance and kleptocracy can be factors which prevent development in Africa. In Nigeria, up to $3 billion was lost due to theft by its dictator. **Social factors:** • HIV/AIDS – the AIDS epidemic has had a huge impact on development. Over 20 million Africans have HIV/AIDS with 1.5 million people dying each year. The virus disproportionately affects younger people with half of those infected being under 25 years of age • HIV/AIDS places a huge cost on countries. Hospitals and health services cannot cope with the epidemic • reduction in life expectancy of up to 20 years and in some countries over 30% of the population are infected • impact of malaria – estimated that the impact of malaria accounts for $12 billion per year. WHO estimates that malaria accounts for up to 50% of hospital admissions • poor educational attainment holds development back, debt repayment has affected educational provision with free education ending in many of the countries. *Any other valid point that meets the criteria described in the general marking instructions for this kind of question.* **Possible approaches to answering this question:** **Response 1:** One factor that can affect development in Africa is the crippling debt that many African countries have to governments and organisations such as the World Bank and the IMF. African countries owe over $200 billion and debt repayments often mean that many social programmes such as Health and Education projects suffer due to countries having to pay back the debt. **(Total 2 marks – 2 marks KU).** **Response 2:** No single factor can be seen as being the most important factor in preventing development in Africa. Their importance depends on the region or country affected and the impact of a particular factor on development. For example, in countries where conflict and civil war exists such as Angola, development and reconstruction can be hindered due to conflict affecting population displacement and crop cultivation **(1 mark KU, 1 mark evaluation)**. However, in areas without conflict but a high number of HIV/AIDS infections then this health factor can inhibit growth and development. Therefore, we can see that the importance of a factor depends on location and individual circumstances of the region or country affected **(1 mark analysis, 1 mark evaluation).** **(Total 4 marks – 1 mark KU, 1 mark analysis, 2 marks evaluation).**

Question		General Marking Instructions for this type of question	Max mark	Specific Marking Instructions for this question
5.	(c)	(continued)		**Response 3:** When studying the impact and effects of different factors on development in Africa, it is clear that many factors are linked and can affect each other. For example, the growth of HIV/AIDS in parts of Africa can seriously affect the economic performance of a country and many days employment are lost through death, illness or caring for family members who are ill **(1 mark KU, 1 mark analysis)**. This also puts a financial strain on health services and budgets as they struggle to cope with the high cost of paying for medicines and treating HIV patients. Also, in Africa many of the victims are young and many are nurses or teachers too which means that countries struggle to employ new teachers and nurses in order to replace those who have fallen victim to the virus **(1 mark KU, 1 mark analysis)**. This shows that many factors are interlinked and have an impact on not just development but also impacting upon other factors that prevent development. Therefore, there is a vicious cycle of problems and issues all affecting growth and development in countries such as Botswana in Africa **(2 marks evaluation)**. **(Total 6 marks — 2 marks KU, 2 marks analysis, 2 marks evaluation).** **Credit reference to aspects of the following:** **World Issue: International terrorism:** **Causes of terrorism:** • social, economic and political causes of terrorism • terrorist groups and perpetrators of terrorist acts often have different motivations • there does not appear to be a single factor that explains the motivation for individual to collective terrorist acts • some who engage in terrorist acts may solely be doing so for personal reasons such as hate or for a desire for power • some carry out terrorist acts due to psychological reasons eg Dylann Roof's mass shooting in the USA • political motivation — if democratic rights and solutions are not available as a way of settling disputes, or allowing the disadvantaged to have a say or a voice some may resort to violent acts. Anders Breivik's views on White Nationalism and immigration showed some sort of political motivation • group psychology explanations for terrorist acts have had some success in trying to look at the processes within a group dynamic to help explain terrorist acts • some terrorist groups will see their use of terrorism as a way of imposing their ideologies onto a nation or a people. Ideologies can encompass religious or political philosophies and ideas eg the IRA and Tamil Tigers in Sri Lanka. Some could argue that ISIL are motivated by a politico-religious ideology • there is also evidence that socio-economic conditions can often lay the ground and sow the seeds for terrorist recruitment, particularly in the developing world. Economic deprivation, poverty and income inequality can make it easier for terrorist organisations to recruit followers. For example, in Gaza and the Palestinian Territories.

Question		General Marking Instructions for this type of question	Max mark	Specific Marking Instructions for this question
5.	(d)	An analysis mark should be awarded where a candidate uses their knowledge and understanding/a source, to identify relevant components (eg of an idea, theory, argument, etc) and clearly show at least one of the following: • links between different components • links between component(s) and the whole • links between components(s) and related concepts • similarities and contradictions • consistency and inconsistency • different views/interpretations • possible consequences/ implications • the relative importance of components • understanding of underlying order or structure. Evaluation involves making judgements based on criteria, drawing conclusions on the extent to which a view is supported by the evidence; counter-arguments including possible alternative interpretations; the overall impact/ significance of the factors when taken together; the relative importance of factors in relation to the context. Credit responses that make reference to: • national and international attempts to solve a given issue • the extent to which attempts have been successful • the extent to which attempts have had limited success • analysis and balanced comment of the extent of success in tackling a given issue • provide a clear, coherent line of argument. Up to **8 marks** for KU (description, explanation and exemplification) and up to **12 marks** for analytical/ evaluative comments. Award up to **6 marks** per point. Candidates may make reference to any world issues the impact of which extends beyond the boundaries of any single country. This impact may be regional or global in scale. Where a candidate makes more analytical/evaluative points than are required to gain the maximum allocation of 4 marks, these can be credited as knowledge and understanding marks provided they meet the criteria for this.	20	*Candidates can be credited in a number of ways up to a* ***maximum of 20 marks.*** **Credit reference to aspects of the following:** **World Issue: International terrorism:** • national and international attempts to resolve international terrorism in relation to military, humanitarian and financial actions • regional and international attempts to resolve terrorism by organisations such as the UN, NATO, the EU and African Union • UK counter terrorism strategy to deal with terrorism in UK with the aim to disrupt financial supply networks and ISIL volunteers leaving UK and joining ISIL in Syria. The Office for Security and Counter Terrorism and the Treasury are jointly responsible for UKs Counter Terrorist Finance Strategy • increased legislation including The Terrorism Asset Freezing Act 2010 and Al Qaeda Asset Freezing Regulations 2011 give police forces the power to freeze bank accounts of those suspected of terrorist involvement • increase in finance for community work schemes in areas of high Muslim UK populations to counter growth of extremism • UK humanitarian schemes using DFID to lead the UK humanitarian response in areas of high ISIL recruitment such as Iraq etc totalling around £60 million • UK military attempts to resolve terrorism. Training and equipping of Kurdish Peshmerga to take fight to ISIL. Also, use of air strikes to disrupt ISIL positions • United Nations. The United Nations Global Counter Terrorism Strategy intends to enhance national, regional and international efforts to combat terrorism. Its main aims are: tackle the conditions that cause terrorism, prevent and combat terrorism, respect human rights for all and rule of law while countering terrorism • the UN can also use peace keeping troops in those areas rife with terrorist activities and recruitment eg Libya and involvement in Iraq and the wider Middle East • European Union. After attacks on London and Madrid, EU established a Counter Terrorism Coordinator to oversee the EU member states' responses to terrorism. Other measures include the Data Retention Directive which allows governments to keep and monitor telephone records for up to a year as well as insisting that banks investigate and report all transactions of more than €15,000. The EUs counter terrorism strategy also includes the Prevent, Protect, Pursue and Respond initiative • NATO. Following end of the Cold War, NATO refocused its main purpose to one of tackling the threat of global terrorism and to create strategies that deal with international security. Operation Active Endeavour is NATO's main anti-terrorist strategy. It aims to disrupt activity in the Mediterranean Sea and to monitor and intercept suspect boats and vessels • the Defence Against Terrorism Programme of Work (DATPOW) attempts to use modern technology to strengthen the fight against terrorism. Also, sharing of terrorism-related information between member states has increased and is much more detailed and effective than it previously was • NATO has also created their own Response Force of land, air and maritime Special Forces to react and respond to threats to international security very quickly • African Union established an African Centre for the study and research on terrorism which advises and supports African regimes in tackling terrorist threats and activities. The AU also promotes enhanced cooperation and information sharing on terrorist groups, their activities and intended targets. *Any other valid point that meets the criteria described in the general marking instructions for this kind of question.*

Question		General Marking Instructions for this type of question	Max mark	Specific Marking Instructions for this question
5.	(d)	(continued)		**Possible approaches to answering this question — International terrorism.** **Response 1:** The European Union has attempted to tackle international terrorism by introducing directives that allow EU member governments to retain telephone records for up to a year as well as sharing information among member states. One such example is Prevent, Protect, Pursue and Respond Strategy **(2 marks KU).** **(Total 2 marks — 2 marks KU).** **Response 2:** The European Union has attempted to tackle international terrorism by introducing directives that allow EU member governments to retain telephone records for up to a year as well as sharing information among member states. One such example is Prevent, Protect, Pursue and Respond Strategy **(2 marks KU).** However, critics say that the EU's approach does not tackle the root cause of terrorism. Critics also state that the number of attacks on EU soil is rising, eg attacks in Paris, Belgium and Berlin. This indicates that the EU has not been effective as attacks are not only continuing, they are increasing in frequency **(1 mark analysis, 1 mark evaluation).** **(Total 4 marks — 2 marks KU, 1 mark analysis, 1 mark evaluation).** **Response 3:** Some argue that the United Nations has been moderately successful in tackling international terrorism. They have the power of the international community behind them as well as the power to impose financial or political sanctions on countries that are seen to support terrorist groups **(1 mark KU, 1 mark evaluation).** They have been successful at keeping the peace in trouble spots around the world where terrorism could be an issue. However, five permanent members having a veto means that they can often stop criticism of their actions or their allies' actions which could, in turn, lead to increased anger by groups and, possibly, increased terror attacks **(2 marks analysis).** For example, the US use of the veto to stop criticism of Israel in terms of their treatment of Palestine in the disputed territories has led to increased attacks in Israel by Hamas and other groups, this shows that the actions of UN members can sometimes lead to further terrorist attacks rather than decreasing them **(1 mark KU, 1 mark evaluation).** **(Total 6 marks — 2 marks KU, 2 marks analysis, 2 marks evaluation).** **Credit reference to aspects of the following:** **World Issue: Development in Africa:** • the work of NGOs such as Christian Aid, Save the Children, Oxfam, Action Aid, etc. NGOs will target specific groups and provide specialist services • different types of aid and some of the problems associated with Bilateral Aid, Tied Aid and Food Aid • Food Aid can often be misdirected by corrupt regimes. Short term solution which doesn't address long term causes of the issue • Tied Aid often favours donor country rather than receiving country • success of campaign against Tied Aid and benefits of it: increased competition with local companies often benefiting which aids local economy providing more jobs and increased spending

Question		General Marking Instructions for this type of question	Max mark	Specific Marking Instructions for this question
5.	(d)	(continued)		• African Union aims to encourage economic cooperation and promoting rights of African nations to run their own affairs. AU often criticised for being too bureaucratic and slow to respond to crises. AU poorly financed which limits its scope to achieve its aims • progress towards Millennium Development Goals. Progress is slow and inconsistent • work of UN and its agencies: UNICEF, WHO, FAO, WFP. UN has an excellent track record of providing assistance. However, underfunding and countries cutting back on voluntary contributions has meant restrictions or cancellations of key projects. UN's work is often undermined by corrupt regimes and bad governance • EU: committed to Cotonou Agreement. Criticism that terms of agreement weighed too much in favour of EU. Also criticised for being too slow and inefficient with aid being misspent • DFID: UK is the largest contributor to an International Development Association, however UK's overall contribution of 0.4% of GDP is lower than the 0.7% that UK is committed to. **Possible approaches to answering this question — Development in Africa.** **Response 1:** One attempt at tackling development in Africa is through the work of the UN. They have many specialist agencies that aim to tackle specific issues. For example, UNICEF works to improve the health and well-being of mothers and babies and the World Food Programme aims to improve farming practices in the developing world **(2 marks KU).** **(Total 2 marks — 2 marks KU).** **Response 2:** One attempt at tackling development in Africa is through the work of the UN. They have many specialist agencies that aim to tackle specific issues. For example, UNICEF works to improve the health and well-being of mothers and babies and the World Food Programme aims to improve farming practices in the developing world **(2 marks KU).** UNICEF has been successful as they are involved in 45 African nations and millions of mothers and babies have benefited from the work of UNICEF. However, the scale of the problem and the ongoing AIDS crisis makes it particularly difficult for UNICEF to be fully successful. Therefore, they have had mixed fortunes in tackling the issue **(1 mark analysis, 1 mark evaluation).** **(Total 4 marks — 2 marks KU, 1 mark analysis, 1 mark evaluation).**

HIGHER MODERN STUDIES 2018 SPECIMEN QUESTION PAPER

General marking principles for Higher Modern Studies Paper 1 (from 2019)

Marking principles for each question type

For each of the question types the following provides an overview of marking principles.

The extended-response questions used in this paper are:

- discuss ... **20 marks**
- to what extent ... **20 marks**
- evaluate ... **12 marks**
- analyse ... **12 marks**

Extended response (12 or 20 marks)

For 12 mark questions, award **up to 8 marks** for knowledge and understanding (description, explanation and exemplification). Award the remaining marks for the demonstration of higher-order skills of analysis **or** evaluation. Where a candidate makes more analytical/evaluative points than are required to gain the **maximum allocation of 4 marks**, award as knowledge and understanding marks provided they meet the criteria for this.

For 20 mark questions, award **up to 8 marks** for knowledge and understanding (description, explanation and exemplification). Award the remaining marks for the demonstration of higher-order skills of analysis **and** evaluation **and** structured argument. Where a candidate makes more analytical/evaluative points than are required to gain the **maximum allocation of 6 marks**, award as knowledge and understanding marks provided they meet the criteria for this.

In *Section 1 — Democracy in Scotland and the United Kingdom* and *Section 2 — Social Issues in the United Kingdom*, award marks where candidates' responses refer to Scotland only, to the United Kingdom only, or to both Scotland and the United Kingdom.

- **Discuss** questions
  Candidates communicate ideas and information on the issue in the statement. Candidates gain marks for analysing and evaluating different views of the statement or viewpoint.
- **To what extent** questions
  Candidates gain marks for analysing the issue in the question and coming to a conclusion or conclusions which involve an evaluative judgement, which is likely to be quantitative in nature.
- **Evaluate** questions
  Candidates gain marks for making a judgement based on criteria; for determining the value of something.
- **Analyse** questions
  Candidates gain marks for identifying parts of an issue, the relationship between these parts and their relationships with the whole; and for drawing out and relating implications.

Higher Modern Studies marking grid for 20 mark questions (KU = 8 marks; analysis/evaluation = 12 marks)

	1 mark	2 marks	3 marks	4 marks	5–6 marks
Range of relevant knowledge Accurate, relevant, up to date.	One relevant aspect of the issue given with some description.	Two relevant aspects of the issue given with some description **or** one relevant aspect covered with detailed and accurate description.	One relevant aspect of the issue with detailed and accurate description **and** one relevant aspect with some description.	At least two relevant aspects with detailed and accurate descriptions which should include the key aspects of the issue.	
Quality of explanation/ exemplification of the issue Award up to the **maximum of 8 marks** available for KU.	Some explanation of one aspect of the issue **or** relevant exemplification.	Some explanation of two relevant aspects of the issue **or** detailed explanation of one aspect of the question which may include relevant exemplification.	Detailed explanation of one relevant aspect of the issue with relevant exemplification **and** some explanation of one aspect of the question.	Full explanation of at least two aspects, which relate closely to the key aspects of the question **and** extended, relevant, accurate and up-to-date exemplification.	
Analysis Comments that identify relationships/implications, explore different views or establish consequences and implications. Award up to **6 marks.***	One relevant and accurate analytical comment.	One relevant and accurate analytical comment that is justified **or** exemplified **or** two different relevant and accurate analytical comments.	One developed relevant and accurate analytical comment that is justified **and** exemplified; this should relate closely to a key aspect of the question.	One extended, accurate and justified analytical comment of an insightful nature which relates closely to the key aspects of the question and is exemplified.	At least two developed relevant and accurate analytical comments that are justified **and** exemplified. These should relate closely to the question and may be linked for **6 marks.**
Structure Develops a consistent and clear line of argument. Award up to **2 marks.**	Clear structure that addresses the issue identified in the question.	Structure that clarifies the issue, presents evidence and develops a clear and consistent line or argument.			
Conclusions Evaluative comments which make a judgement(s) and or reach a conclusion(s) which address the key issues in the question. Award up to **4 marks.***	One conclusion that addresses a key issue in the question.	One extended and balanced conclusion that addresses a key issue in the question **or** two conclusions that address key issues in the question.	One extended and balanced conclusion that is justified and directly addresses the key issue(s) in the question **or** two balanced conclusions that address the key issues in the question, one of which is extended.	One extended and balanced insightful conclusion that is justified and directly addresses the central aspects of the question **and** which considers a range of viewpoints.	

*Where a candidate makes more analytical and/or evaluative points required to gain the maximum allocation of marks, award these as knowledge and understanding marks, provided they meet the criteria for this.

Note: answers to **20 mark** questions should demonstrate at least two relevant aspects of knowledge and provide detailed analysis and evaluation.

For **full marks** in the KU aspect of the question (8/8), a response **must** include a range of points, have detailed explanation, and include a range of accurate exemplification.

Award **a maximum of 6 marks** (from 8 for KU) if there is no exemplification.

For **full marks** (20/20), a response **must** be structured, include a range of points, have detailed explanation, include a range of accurate and relevant exemplification and contain extended analysis and evaluation.

Higher Modern Studies marking grid for 12 mark questions (KU = 8 marks; analysis/evaluation = 4 marks)

	1 mark	2 marks	3 marks	4 marks
Range of relevant knowledge Accurate, relevant, up to date.	One relevant aspect of the issue given with some description.	Two relevant aspects of the issue given with some description **or** one relevant aspect covered with detailed and accurate description.	One relevant aspect of the issue with detailed and accurate description **and** one relevant aspect with some description.	At least two relevant aspects with detailed and accurate descriptions which should include the key aspects of the issue.
Quality of explanation/ exemplification of the issue Award up to the **maximum of 8 marks** available for KU.	Some explanation of one aspect of the issue **or** relevant exemplification.	Some explanation of two relevant aspects of the issue **or** detailed explanation of one aspect of the question which may include relevant exemplification.	Detailed explanation of one relevant aspect of the issue with relevant exemplification **and** some explanation of one aspect of the question.	Full explanation of at least two aspects, which relate closely to the key aspects of the question **and** extended, relevant, accurate and up-to-date exemplification.
Analysis/evaluation Comments that identify relationships, implications and make judgements. Award up to **4 marks.***	One relevant and accurate analytical or evaluative comment.	One relevant and accurate analytical or evaluative comment that is justified **or** exemplified **or** two different relevant and accurate analytical/ evaluative comments.	One developed relevant and accurate analytical or evaluative comment that is justified **and** exemplified; this should relate closely to a key aspect of the question.	One extended, accurate and justified analytical or evaluative comment of an insightful nature which relates closely to the key aspects of the question and is exemplified.

*Where a candidate makes more analytical/evaluative points than are required to gain the maximum allocation of marks, award these as knowledge and understanding marks, provided they meet the criteria for this.

Note: answers to **12 mark** questions should demonstrate at least two relevant aspects of knowledge.

For **full marks** in the KU aspect of the question (8/8), a response **must** include a range of points, have detailed explanation and include a range of accurate exemplification.

Award **a maximum of 6 marks** (from 8 for KU) if there is no accurate or relevant exemplification.

For **full marks** (12/12), a response **must** include a range of points, have detailed explanation, include a range of accurate and relevant exemplification and analysis or evaluation.

Section 1 – Democracy in Scotland and the United Kingdom

Question		General Marking Instructions	Max marks	Specific Marking Instructions for this question
1.	(a)	Award an analysis mark where candidates use their knowledge and understanding or a source to identify relevant components (for example, of an idea, theory, argument) and clearly show at least one of the following: • links between different components • links between component(s) and the whole • links between component(s) and related concepts • similarities and contradictions • consistency and inconsistency • different views or interpretations • possible consequences or implications • the relative importance of components • understanding of underlying order or structure. Evaluation involves making judgements based on criteria, drawing conclusions on the extent to which a view is supported by the evidence; counter-arguments including possible alternative interpretations; the overall impact or significance of the factors when taken together; the relative importance of factors in relation to the context. Award up to **8 marks** for KU (description, explanation and exemplification) and up to **12 marks** for analytical or evaluative comments. Award up to **6 marks** per point. Award up to **full marks** if candidates answer within a Scottish context only, a UK context only, or refer to both Scotland and the UK as appropriate. Where candidates make more analytical and/or evaluative points than are required to gain the maximum allocation of marks, award these as knowledge and understanding marks provided they meet the criteria for this.	20	Candidates can gain marks in a number of ways **up to a maximum of 20 marks.** Award marks where candidates refer to aspects of the following: • analysis and evaluation of the influence of age in voting in recent elections and referenda • different factors other than age that influence voting behaviour • implications of different factors influencing voting behaviour. Candidates may refer to: • media • social class • gender • geographical location or residence • ethnicity • party leader competence and image • issues. *Any other valid point that meets the criteria described in the general marking instructions for this type of question.* **Possible approaches to answering this question:** **Response 1** Age is an important factor which will affect the way a person votes. Young voters are classed as 18–24 year olds followed by categorising voters from 25–34 year olds and 35–44 year olds. A majority of voters in all three of these age groups voted Labour in the 2017 General Election. **(1 mark KU)** These groups are more likely to agree with Labour party policies on issues such as the NHS, education, taxation and the welfare state. **(1 mark analysis)** Among older voters in the 45–54 year old, 55–64 year old and over-65s age groups, there was a majority vote for the Conservatives. **(1 mark KU)** So voters are more likely to be socialist when they are young but become more conservative as they get older. **(1 mark evaluation)** **Total 4 marks – 2 marks KU, 1 mark analysis, 1 mark evaluation.** **Response 2** Age is a factor that can determine voting behaviour. Historically, elections show that young voters are more likely to vote Labour than Conservative. **(1 mark KU)** For instance in the 2017 UK General Election 62% of 18–24 year olds voted for Labour compared to 27% who voted Conservative. **(1 mark KU)** The young tend to vote for Labour due to the feeling that the Labour party and their policies represent a challenge to authority and the establishment which younger people are more likely to find attractive. **(1 mark analysis)** In contrast, older voters are more likely to vote Conservative. 61% of over 65 year olds voted Conservative compared to 25% for Labour in the 2017 General Election. **(1 mark KU)** The elderly are more inclined to vote Conservative because their policies on issues like pensions and tax are more likely to benefit them and also because the elderly are more likely to be opposed to radical social changes, which the Conservative party's policies are in line with. **(1 mark analysis)** 2017's General Election shows that the Conservatives won the most seats which suggests it is the votes of the elderly which are most influential. **(1 mark evaluation)** **Total 6 marks – 3 marks KU, 2 marks analysis, 1 mark evaluation.**

<table>
<tr><th colspan="2">Question</th><th>General Marking Instructions</th><th>Max marks</th><th>Specific Marking Instructions for this question</th></tr>
<tr><td>1.</td><td>(a)</td><td>(continued)</td><td></td><td>Response 3
Although age can be a factor in voting, how someone votes is often influenced by their views on political parties, their policies and their leaders. The media, including newspapers, television and radio as well as new media such as social networking, plays an important role in shaping how a leader or a political party and their policies are portrayed. (1 mark KU) Parties such as the Labour party, the Conservatives and the SNP clearly believe that the media plays a part in influencing how people vote as they spend a lot of money on spin doctors, media monitoring units and rapid rebuttal teams to ensure that the public are aware of their policies. (1 mark KU) This level of commitment shows that the media can be a key factor in influencing voting behaviour. (1 mark evaluation)

Total 3 marks — 2 marks KU, 1 mark evaluation.

Where candidates provide answers which deal only with the influence of age, award a maximum of 12 marks.</td></tr>
<tr><td></td><td>(b)</td><td>Award an analysis mark where candidates use their knowledge and understanding or a source to identify relevant components (for example, of an idea, theory, argument) and clearly show at least one of the following:
• links between different components
• links between component(s) and the whole
• links between component(s) and related concepts
• similarities and contradictions
• consistency and inconsistency
• different views or interpretations
• possible consequences/ implications
• the relative importance of components
• understanding of underlying order or structure.

Evaluation involves making judgements based on criteria, drawing conclusions on the extent to which a view is supported by the evidence; counter-arguments including possible alternative interpretations; the overall impact or significance of the factors when taken together; the relative importance of factors in relation to the context.

Award up to 8 marks for KU (description, explanation and exemplification) and up to 12 marks for analytical or evaluative comments.

Award up to 6 marks per point.

Award up to full marks if candidates answer within a Scottish context only, a UK context only, or refer to both Scotland and the UK as appropriate.</td><td>20</td><td>Candidates can gain marks in a number of ways up to a maximum of 20 marks.

Award marks where candidates refer to aspects of the following:
• analysis and evaluation of the positive implications leaving the EU may have for the UK
• analysis and evaluation of the negative implications leaving the EU may have for the UK.

Candidates may refer to:
• soft versus hard Brexit
• sovereignty and legislative autonomy
• border control, freedom of movement and immigration
• human rights issues
• employment law and workers' rights, for example EU Working Time Directive
• security, Europol, European Arrest Warrant
• EURATOM
• single market, customs union, Free Trade
• hard/no-deal Brexit and World Trade Organisation rules
• UK's global influence as part of the EU and influence as a sovereign nation
• UK economic opportunities, for example bilateral trade agreements.

Any other valid point that meets the criteria described in the general marking instructions for this type of question.

Possible approaches to answering this question:

Response 1
Leaving the EU has possible trade benefits for the UK. Brexiteers argue that this will allow the UK to arrange Free Trade deals with individual countries. (1 mark KU) President Trump and Prime Minister Jacinda Ardern of New Zealand have expressed interest to quickly establish post-Brexit trade deals with the UK. (1 mark KU)

Total — 2 marks KU.

Response 2
The UK has voted to leave its largest trading partner and biggest market for its exports. Over 40% of UK exports are to the EU and over 50% of our imports come from EU countries. (1 mark KU) UK Government analysis of the impact of Brexit showed every possible post-Brexit relationship between the UK and the EU will make the UK economically worse off. (1 mark analysis) If the UK ends up with the 'softest' Brexit, its economy will be 2% worse off, a 'softish' Brexit will make the economy 5% worse off, but a 'hard', no-deal Brexit will make the economy 15% worse off over the following 15 years. (1 mark KU) Leaving the EU will therefore damage the UK economically but the degree of this</td></tr>
</table>

Question		General Marking Instructions	Max marks	Specific Marking Instructions for this question
1.	(b)	(continued) Where candidates make more analytical and/or evaluative points than are required to gain the maximum allocation of marks, award these as knowledge and understanding marks provided they meet the criteria for this.		damage will depend on the type of relationship the UK achieves with the EU zone after negotiations, the hardest of Brexits bringing the most damaging outcomes. **(2 marks evaluation)** **Total 5 marks — 2 marks KU, 1 mark analysis, 2 marks evaluation.** **Response 3** By leaving the EU the UK will regain sovereignty and control over its own law and legal affairs. The UK Parliament, Scottish Parliament and the UK Supreme Court will now be the main creators and interpreters of laws in the UK rather than the EU and EU courts whose laws and legal decisions currently override those of the UK. **(2 marks KU)** However, while the UK will regain legal freedom from the EU courts there are problems if UK laws start to differ too much from the laws of the EU zone. Many of our human rights, working rights, and food and safety standards are based on EU laws. There is a fear that human rights and workers' rights may be removed to make it easier for businesses to operate in the UK and make profits. **(1 mark KU, 1 mark analysis)** If we introduce lower standards of safety in our products or food we will find it difficult to sell them into the EU market as they will not comply with their standards, which could be damaging to our economy, especially to small and medium-sized enterprises. **(1 mark analysis)** So while it would be good to regain sovereignty, it would cause some economic problems. **(1 mark evaluation)** **Total 6 marks — 3 marks KU, 2 marks analysis, 1 mark evaluation.** Where candidates provide answers which deal with only one side of the Brexit debate, award **a maximum of 12 marks.**
	(c)	Award an analysis mark where candidates use their knowledge and understanding or a source to identify relevant components (for example, of an idea, theory, argument) and clearly show at least one of the following: • links between different components • links between component(s) and the whole • links between component(s) and related concepts • similarities and contradictions • consistency and inconsistency • different views or interpretations • possible consequences or implications • the relative importance of components • understanding of underlying order or structure. Evaluation involves making judgements based on criteria, drawing conclusions on the extent to which a view is supported by the evidence; counter-arguments including possible alternative interpretations; the overall impact or significance of the factors when taken together; the relative importance of factors in relation to the context.	20	Candidates can gain marks in a number of ways **up to a maximum of 20 marks.** Award marks where candidates refer to aspects of the following: • analysis and evaluation of the Scottish or UK legislative processes and opportunities for scrutiny of the government • provide balanced analytical/evaluative comment on the ways parliamentary representatives can check government power. Candidates may refer to: **Scotland** • First Minister's questions • work of committees • questions to individual ministers • voting • type of government can affect effectiveness — minority, majority or coalition • size of government majority • backbench rebellion • debates and motions • role and power of the whips • decision time. **UK** • Prime Minister's questions • select committees • questions to individual ministers • role of House of Lords as amending chamber • power of the whips • type of government — minority, majority and coalition • size of government majority • backbench rebellion • early day motions/ten minute bills • voting • Salisbury Convention for policies in government manifesto.

<table>
<tr><th colspan="2">Question</th><th>General Marking Instructions</th><th>Max marks</th><th>Specific Marking Instructions for this question</th></tr>
<tr><td>1.</td><td>(c)</td><td>(continued)

Award up to 8 marks for KU (description, explanation and exemplification) and up to 12 marks for analytical or evaluative comments.

Award up to 6 marks per point.

Award up to full marks if candidates answer within a Scottish context only, a UK context only, or refer to both Scotland and the UK as appropriate.

Where candidates make more analytical and/or evaluative points than are required to gain the maximum allocation of marks, award these as knowledge and understanding marks provided they meet the criteria for this.</td><td></td><td>Any other valid point that meets the criteria described in the general marking instructions for this type of question.

Possible approaches to answering this question:

Response 1
In the Scottish Parliament MSPs can hold the Scottish Government to account through asking questions of the First Minister, Nicola Sturgeon, at First Minister's Questions every Thursday. The leader of the opposition, the Conservative party leader Ruth Davidson, gets to ask six questions which force the government to defend and explain their actions.

Total — 2 marks KU.

Response 2
Committees in the Scottish Parliament are made up of MSPs and have considerable powers to scrutinise the legislation of the Scottish Government, in areas such as health and education. (1 mark KU) As the Scottish Parliament has only one chamber, committees play a stronger role in checking the actions of government in Scotland than they do in other parliaments which are bicameral like the UK Parliament. (1 mark evaluation) However, the membership of committees reflects the size of the parties in parliament so the SNP are more likely to be the biggest group on each committee and are more likely to hold the convenorship of committees. (1 mark analysis) This gives the SNP and their government considerable power to overcome scrutiny by other MSPs and parties. (1 mark evaluation)

Total 4 marks — 1 mark KU, 1 mark analysis, 2 marks evaluation.

Response 3
As elections for the Scottish Parliament are based on the Additional Members System it is less likely to provide an overall majority for the governing party. Since 2016's Scottish Parliamentary elections the SNP has had to govern as a minority due to the fact they only gained 63 of the 129 MSPs. (2 marks KU) This means they need the support of other parties or MSPs to pass their legislation. (1 mark analysis) In 2017 the SNP minority government needed the support of the Green Party's six MSPs to pass their budget. As a result the Green Party was able to get some concessions from the SNP including keeping the 40% income tax rate and getting an extra £160 million for local councils. (1 mark KU, 1 mark analysis) This shows that when a government does not have an overall majority it is easier for parliament and other parties to hold them to account and limit what they can do. (1 mark evaluation)

Total 6 marks — 3 marks KU, 2 marks analysis, 1 mark evaluation.</td></tr>
</table>

Section 2 — Social Issues in the United Kingdom

<table>
<tr><th colspan="2">Question</th><th>General Marking Principles</th><th>Max marks</th><th>Specific Marking Instructions for this question</th></tr>
<tr><td>2.</td><td>(a)</td><td>Award an analysis mark where candidates use their knowledge and understanding or a source to identify relevant components (for example, of an idea, theory, argument) and clearly show at least one of the following:
• links between different components
• links between component(s) and the whole
• links between component(s) and related concepts
• similarities and contradictions
• consistency and inconsistency
• different views or interpretations
• possible consequences or implications
• the relative importance of components
• understanding of underlying order or structure.

Evaluation involves making judgements based on criteria, drawing conclusions on the extent to which a view is supported by the evidence; counter-arguments including possible alternative interpretations; the overall impact or significance of the factors when taken together; the relative importance of factors in relation to the context.

Award up to 8 marks for KU (description, explanation and exemplification) and up to 12 marks for analytical or evaluative comments.

Award up to 6 marks per point.

Award up to full marks if candidates answer within a Scottish context only, a UK context only, or refer to both Scotland and the UK as appropriate.

Where candidates make more analytical and/or evaluative points than are required to gain the maximum allocation of marks, award these as knowledge and understanding marks provided they meet the criteria for this.</td><td>20</td><td>Candidates can gain marks in a number of ways up to a maximum of 20 marks.

Where candidates' responses consider only one cause of inequality, award a maximum of 12 marks.

Award marks where candidates refer to aspects of the following:
• make reference to causes of economic inequality
• provide balanced analytical/evaluative comments referring to causes of economic inequality.

Candidates may refer to:
• employment/unemployment status
• educational inequalities
• social class inequalities
• gender/ethnic inequalities
• regional inequalities
• capitalist economics
• austerity policies and welfare reform
• taxation
• housing
• concentration of wealth among top 1%, for example ownership of stocks and shares.

Any other valid point that meets the criteria described in the general marking instructions for this type of question.

Possible approaches to answering this question:

Response 1
Whether someone has a job as well as the type of job they have is a key cause of inequality. The unemployed are on benefits which are designed to provide the minimum amount required to get by. Other workers may only have part-time work earning the minimum wage (£7·83) which means that their income and level of pay is much lower than the average wage. (2 marks KU) As a result, low-income earners may have a lower quality of life, poorer diet, and suffer more stress and anxiety. (1 mark analysis)

Total 3 marks — 2 marks KU, 1 mark analysis.

Response 2
The housing market is widening the wealth gap across the UK between different generations and regions of the country. This gap is growing between younger and older generations due to the inability of the young to be able to afford or save the large deposits required to gain a mortgage for increasingly more expensive house prices. (2 marks KU) Younger generations therefore do not benefit as much from the wealth that home owning generates as the value of a house can increase over time. (1 mark evaluation) The housing market in London and the South of England, although more expensive, is also more profitable than other areas of the UK. (1 mark KU)

Total 4 marks — 3 marks KU, 1 mark evaluation.</td></tr>
</table>

<table>
<tr><th colspan="2">Question</th><th>General Marking Principles</th><th>Max marks</th><th>Specific Marking Instructions for this question</th></tr>
<tr><td>2.</td><td>(a)</td><td>(continued)</td><td></td><td>Response 3
Education and educational attainment continues to be the biggest cause of inequality in the UK. The educational system of the UK supports and reinforces inequality within the UK. (1 mark evaluation) Although only 7% of the population go to private school they make up almost 75% of judges, over 70% of top military personnel, and over 50% of journalists and senior civil servants. (1 mark KU) One school, Eton, has even produced 19 of the UK's Prime Ministers. (1 mark KU) This elite, privately-educated group dominate the law, politics, military and media in the UK where the rules work to their advantage. (1 mark analysis) The privately-educated are also more likely to go to university and to the best universities in the UK such as Oxford and Cambridge. Graduates typically earn £12,000 more per year than non-graduates, equivalent to £500,000 more over a working lifetime, but this earnings gap is even bigger for Oxbridge graduates who on average earn £400,000 more than other university graduates over their working lifetime. (2 marks KU) This shows that the income gap between the privately-educated and the rest is a major factor in inequality within the UK. (1 mark evaluation)
Total 7 marks — 4 marks KU, 1 mark analysis, 2 marks evaluation.

Note: apply the 6 marks maximum for response 3 as it only addresses one point (private education).</td></tr>
<tr><td></td><td>(b)</td><td>Award an analysis mark where candidates use their knowledge and understanding or a source to identify relevant components (for example, of an idea, theory, argument) and clearly show at least one of the following:
• links between different components
• links between component(s) and the whole
• links between component(s) and related concepts
• similarities and contradictions
• consistency and inconsistency
• different views or interpretations
• possible consequences or implications
• the relative importance of components
• understanding of underlying order or structure.

Evaluation involves making judgements based on criteria, drawing conclusions on the extent to which a view is supported by the evidence; counter-arguments including possible alternative interpretations; the overall impact or significance of the factors when taken together; the relative importance of factors in relation to the context.

Award up to 8 marks for KU (description, explanation and exemplification) and up to 12 marks for analytical or evaluative comments.</td><td>20</td><td>Candidates can gain marks in a number of ways up to a maximum of 20 marks.

Award marks where candidates refer to aspects of the following:
• government policies that have targeted social and economic inequalities
• provide analytical/evaluative comment on the effectiveness of government policies in reducing social and economic inequalities.

Candidates may refer to:
• the benefits system — Universal Credit, Tax Credits, Jobseeker's Allowance, Child Benefit, State Pensions
• National Minimum Wage (NMW) and the Living Wage campaign
• the impact of austerity measures and government cuts to welfare
• the Equality Act 2010 and reference to Equality and Human Rights Commission reports
• the NHS and policies to reduce health inequality; the smoking ban (2006); free prescription charges; recommendations of Equally Well report; minimum alcohol prices.

Any other valid point that meets the criteria described in the general marking instructions for this type of question.

Possible approaches to answering this question:

Response 1
One policy introduced to tackle inequalities in wealth is the National Minimum Wage (NMW) which was introduced in 1999 as a way of tackling poverty among low-paid workers. (1 mark KU) At the time it was effective in reducing economic inequalities as it raised the pay of 1·3 million workers. Furthermore, according to the Low Pay Commission, 2 million workers have benefited from recent increases in the NMW, significantly 75% of these are women. This shows that people are earning more and that government attempts to tackle wealth inequality through the NMW have been partly effective in reducing low income. (2 marks evaluation) However, it is now argued that the NMW is not sufficient to meet minimum living standards. According to research by the Joseph Rowntree Foundation, in 2015 single people needed to earn at least £17,000 to achieve a minimum income standard, while couples with two children needed to earn at least £20,000 each. (1 mark KU, 1 mark analysis)
Total 5 marks — 2 marks KU, 1 mark analysis, 2 marks evaluation.</td></tr>
</table>

<table>
<tr><th colspan="2">Question</th><th>General Marking Principles</th><th>Max marks</th><th>Specific Marking Instructions for this question</th></tr>
<tr><td>2.</td><td>(b)</td><td>(continued)

Award up to 6 marks per point.

Award up to full marks if candidates answer within a Scottish context only, a UK context only, or refer to both Scotland and the UK as appropriate.

Where candidates make more analytical and/or evaluative points than are required to gain the maximum allocation of marks, award these as knowledge and understanding marks provided they meet the criteria for this.</td><td></td><td>Response 2
The UK Government has recently reformed the benefit system and introduced the Universal Credit which brings together into one payment previous benefits and tax credits such as Jobseeker's Allowance, Employment and Support Allowance and Working Tax Credits. (1 mark KU) This was introduced to reduce the number of people trapped in benefits by increasing the amount people in low-paid work can claim. (1 mark KU) The government thinks that 3·1 million households will be entitled to claim more, in particular working couples with children will benefit. (1 mark analysis)

Total 3 marks — 2 marks KU, 1 mark analysis.

Response 3
The UK Government has tried to reduce social inequalities by introducing the Equality Act of 2010. This gives greater powers to people facing discrimination for a protected characteristic and so helps to reduce inequalities in employment and social life. (1 mark KU) For example, there remains a gender pay gap in the UK, and the Equality Act gives greater powers to women to sue their employer for discrimination in pay. (1 mark KU)

Total — 2 marks KU.</td></tr>
<tr><td></td><td>(c)</td><td>Award an analysis mark where candidates use their knowledge and understanding or a source to identify relevant components (for example of an idea, theory, argument) and clearly show at least one of the following:
• links between different components
• links between component(s) and the whole
• links between component(s) and related concepts
• similarities and contradictions
• consistency and inconsistency
• different views or interpretations
• possible consequences or implications
• underlying order or structure
• understanding of the relative importance of components.

Evaluation involves making judgements based on criteria, drawing conclusions on the extent to which a view is supported by the evidence; counter-arguments including possible alternative interpretations; the overall impact or significance of the factors when taken together; the relative importance of factors in relation to the context.

Award up to 8 marks for KU (description, explanation and exemplification) and up to 12 marks for analytical or evaluative comments.

Award up to 6 marks per point.

Award up to full marks if candidates answer within a Scottish context only, a UK context only, or refer to both Scotland and the UK as appropriate.</td><td>20</td><td>Candidates can gain marks in a number of ways up to a maximum of 20 marks.

Award marks where candidates refer to aspects of the following:
• individualistic and collectivist theories on the causes of crime
• provide analytical/evaluative comments referring to different factors and their relative importance.

Candidates may refer to:
• theories of crime such as individualistic — free will, psychological causes, sociological-functionalism, control theory, labelling, and biological causes of crime
• human nature theory
• social disorganisation/cultural deviance theory
• Robert Merton/Strain theory of crime
• Marxist theory
• Charles Moore/Underclass theory
• Conservative social breakdown theory
• family background, lack of education, poverty and social exclusion, peer pressure, drugs and alcohol.

Award marks where candidate responses refer to links between factors such as drug and/or alcohol abuse, peer influence, family influence, but don't mention theorists specifically.

Any other valid point that meets the criteria described in the general marking instructions for this type of question.

Possible approaches to answering this question:

Response 1
Some people may be more likely to commit crime because of a lack of success in education. This could lead to higher unemployment and therefore people may resort to crime such as theft instead. (1 mark KU)

Total — 1 mark KU.

Response 2
There are many theories as to why people commit crimes; the individualist human nature theory is just one. For example, some people agree with Hobbes' belief that human nature explains crime: we are all essentially selfish and will break the law if given the chance. This could explain looting which took place during the 2011 London riots. (2 marks KU) This, however, cannot explain why many people chose not to take part in looting. Indeed, many people chose not to pursue their own self-interest, instead</td></tr>
</table>

<table>
<tr><th colspan="2">Question</th><th>General Marking Principles</th><th>Max marks</th><th>Specific Marking Instructions for this question</th></tr>
<tr><td>2.</td><td>(c)</td><td>(continued)

Where candidates make more analytical and/or evaluative points than are required to gain the maximum allocation of marks, award these as knowledge and understanding marks provided they meet the criteria for this.</td><td></td><td>they chose to help those whose shops were being looted, so there are limits to the individualist human nature theory.
(1 mark analysis, 1 mark evaluation)

Total 4 marks — 2 marks KU, 1 mark analysis, 1 mark evaluation.

Response 3
One factor that can cause crime is poverty. In areas of high unemployment and social exclusion you are more likely to have higher crime rates. (1 mark KU) There is a clear link between poverty and certain types of crime. For example, Glasgow has the highest level of poverty with six of the 10 poorest constituencies in the UK being in the city. (1 mark KU) It has some of the highest levels of crime such as theft, housebreaking and assault. This shows that there is a clear link between poverty, deprivation and crime. (1 mark analysis) Theorists like Robert Merton argued that as a result of delinquent sub-cultures that can develop in areas like these, people commit crime in order to obtain things they can't afford and to reach society's goals. (1 mark KU) However, Merton's ideas have been criticised as they do not always explain why some people who live in extreme poverty never consider committing a crime. (1 mark analysis) Clearly there is an element of individual choice as to why some people commit crime. (1 mark evaluation)

Total 6 marks — 3 marks KU, 2 marks analysis, 1 mark evaluation.

Award a maximum of 12 marks where candidates consider only one cause of crime.</td></tr>
<tr><td></td><td>(d)</td><td>Award an analysis mark where candidates use their knowledge and understanding or a source to identify relevant components (for example of an idea, theory, argument) and clearly show at least one of the following:
• links between different components
• links between component(s) and the whole
• links between component(s) and related concepts
• similarities and contradictions
• consistency and inconsistency
• different views or interpretations
• possible consequences or implications
• the relative importance of components
• understanding of underlying order or structure.

Evaluation involves making judgements based on criteria, drawing conclusions on the extent to which a view is supported by the evidence; counter-arguments including possible alternative interpretations; the overall impact or significance of the factors when taken together; the relative importance of factors in relation to the context.</td><td>20</td><td>Candidates can gain marks in a number of ways up to a maximum of 20 marks.

Award marks where candidates refer to aspects of the following:
• make reference to non-custodial punishments in the UK or Scotland
• provide analytical/evaluative comments referring to the effectiveness of non-custodial punishments.

Candidates may refer to:
• fines
• Drug Treatment and Testing Orders (DTTOs)
• Community Payback Orders (CPOs)
• Restriction of Liberty Orders (RLOs), for example Home Detention Curfews (HDCs)/electronic tagging
• Anti-Social Behaviour Orders (ASBOs)
• restorative justice
• measures contained in the Criminal Justice and Licensing (Scotland) Act 2010.

Any other valid point that meets the criteria described in the general marking instructions for this type of question.

Possible approaches to answering this question:

Response 1
Drug Treatment and Testing Orders (DTTOs) are sentences available to the courts for offenders with a serious habit of drug misuse which is linked to offending. DTTOs offer support which is aimed at helping drug misusers kick their habits and break the cycle of their offending. (1 mark KU) However, DTTOs have higher rates of reoffending than some prison sentences and low rates of completion. (1 mark evaluation)

Total 2 marks — 1 mark KU, 1 mark evaluation.</td></tr>
</table>

Question		General Marking Principles	Max marks	Specific Marking Instructions for this question
2.	(d)	(continued) Award up to **8 marks** for KU (description, explanation and exemplification) and up to **12 marks** for analytical or evaluative comments. Award up to **6 marks** per point. Award up to **full marks** if candidates answer within a Scottish context only, a UK context only, or refer to both Scotland and the UK as appropriate. Where candidates make more analytical and/or evaluative points than are required to gain the maximum allocation of marks, award these as knowledge and understanding marks provided they meet the criteria for this.		**Response 2** Restorative justice allows victims of crime the opportunity to tell the offender responsible about the harm their actions caused them and how they were affected. In Scotland the Procurator Fiscal can choose to take this course of action if both the victim and perpetrator of a crime agree to it. Dialogue can be face-to-face, by telephone or video-conferencing, or via a third party such as SACRO shuttling information back and forth between the two parties. **(2 marks KU)** Restorative justice is beneficial as it allows victims to address the criminals who harmed them and helps victims or their families gain closure. It is also cheaper than sending people to prison and reduces reoffending by almost 15% for a range of crimes. **(2 marks analysis)** **Total 4 marks — 2 marks KU, 2 marks analysis.** **Response 3** Community Payback Orders (CPOs) were introduced by the Scottish Government in 2011 to allow judges to determine the best course of action for sentencing convicted criminals. CPOs give judges the flexibility to apply a sentence which takes into consideration the offender's criminal record, the risk of them reoffending and their physical and mental health and wellbeing. **(2 marks KU)** Once a Criminal Justice Social Work report has been carried out a judge can then prescribe several courses of action including unpaid work, supervision, treatment for alcohol or drugs or compensation payments to victims. **(1 mark KU)** These community sentences have a reoffending rate of approximately 34% compared to around 45% for those who leave prison. **(1 mark analysis)** The fact that reoffending for CPOs is lower than that for prison suggests that CPOs are effective in reducing crime, however this may not be the case as the type of criminal issued with a CPO is less likely to have committed serious or violent crimes or be what could be called a serial offender or career criminal. **(2 marks analysis)** **Total 6 marks — 3 marks KU, 3 marks analysis.**

Section 3 — International Issues

Question		General Marking Principles	Max marks	Specific Marking Instructions for this question
3.	(a)	Award an analysis mark where candidates use their knowledge and understanding or a source to identify relevant components (for example, of an idea, theory, argument) and clearly show at least one of the following: • links between different components • links between component(s) and the whole • links between component(s) and related concepts • similarities and contradictions • consistency and inconsistency • different views or interpretations • possible consequences or implications • the relative importance of components • understanding of underlying order or structure.	12	Candidates can gain marks in a number of ways **up to a maximum of 12 marks.** Award marks where candidates refer to aspects of the following: • descriptions of political opportunities for people to participate in • an analysis of how different political opportunities can influence decision making. Candidates may refer to: • voting in elections at various levels • membership of political parties • standing as a candidate in elections • party activism • interest group membership • activity protest/direct action. *Any other valid point that meets the criteria described in the general marking instructions for this type of question.*

Question		General Marking Principles	Max marks	Specific Marking Instructions for this question
3.	(a)	(continued) Award up to **8 marks** for KU (description, explanation and exemplification) and up to **4 marks** for analytical comments. Award up to **6 marks** per point. Where candidates make more analytical points than are required to gain the maximum allocation of marks, award these as knowledge and understanding marks provided they meet the criteria for this.		**World power: China** **Possible approach to answering this question:** **Response — China** There are some opportunities for people to participate politically in China such as voting in village elections. These are held every three years and any villager who is aged 18 or above can vote. **(1 mark KU)** At these elections people also have the opportunity to put themselves forward as a candidate for election, however candidates are often selected in a process that some say is not always open and transparent. **(1 mark KU, 1 mark analysis)** However, village committees are limited to decisions on land reform. Decisions regarding more serious issues are made at national or provincial level. **(1 mark analysis)** **Total 4 marks — 2 marks KU, 2 marks analysis.** **World power: USA** **Possible approach to answering this question:** **Response — USA** There are many opportunities for people to participate politically in the USA such as voting during presidential elections. Presidential elections are held every four years and any citizen who is aged 18 or above can vote. **(1 mark KU)** During a presidential election cycle, citizens can join a political party such as the Democrats or the Republicans and vote in the primaries to choose their party's presidential candidate. **(1 mark KU)** **Total — 2 marks KU.** **World power: South Africa** **Possible approach to answering this question:** **Response — South Africa** Many citizens have exercised their political right to protest for and against the rule of the African National Congress in South Africa. In February 2018 during internal party struggles between President Zuma and other ANC leaders, the radical political group Black First Land First organised pro-Zuma demonstrations in Johannesburg using the slogan #HandsOffZuma, while rival demonstrations protested #ZumaMustFall and organised online petitions using this hashtag. **(2 marks KU)** **Total — 2 marks KU.**
	(b)	Evaluation involves making judgements based on criteria, drawing conclusions on the extent to which a view is supported by the evidence; counter-arguments including possible alternative interpretations; the overall impact/ significance of the factors when taken together; the relative importance of factors in relation to the context. Award up to **8 marks** for KU (description, explanation and exemplification) and up to **4 marks** for analytical comments. Award up to **6 marks** per point. Where candidates make more evaluative points than are required to gain the maximum allocation of marks, award these as knowledge and understanding marks provided they meet the criteria for this.	12	Candidates can gain marks in a number of ways **up to a maximum of 12 marks.** Award marks where candidates refer to aspects of the following: • government action aimed at tackling inequality • an evaluation of the successes and/or shortcomings of these actions. Candidates may refer to: • health policies • housing policies • education policies • employment • anti-discrimination • welfare policies. *Any other valid point that meets the criteria described in the general marking instructions for this type of question.*

Question		General Marking Principles	Max marks	Specific Marking Instructions for this question
3.	(b)	(continued)		**World power: Brazil** **Possible approach to answering this question:** **Response — Brazil** One key policy to tackle growing poverty is the welfare strategy of the Bolsa Familia which provides financial support to those families with children living below the poverty line. **(1 mark KU)** The programme has grown rapidly, and in the past 10 years the number of families receiving payments has risen from 3·6 million to 13·8 million, covering nearly a quarter of Brazil's population. **(1 mark KU)** However, the payment is conditional and is only guaranteed if the children are kept in school and get vaccinated. Some also argue the payment is too little to live on, with payments of 70 reais a person to any family below the poverty line of 140 reais a month, hence not really helping end poverty. **(2 marks evaluation)** Furthermore, some Brazilians have reported that they have tried to claim the benefits paid out by Bolsa Familia and have failed to receive any money from the government. Critics claim that this policy has had limited success and non-payment is often down to the corruption of local officials. **(1 mark KU, 1 mark evaluation)** **Total 6 marks — 3 marks KU, 3 marks evaluation.** **World power: USA** **Possible approach to answering this question:** **Response — USA** Before the introduction of the Patient Protection and Affordable Care Act (PPACA), or Obamacare as it was nicknamed, approximately 50 million American citizens did not have health insurance because it was either unaffordable or because employers were reducing the health coverage they provided to workers. To assist the 15% of the population who were not covered by their employers or by US healthcare programs such as Medicaid, Barack Obama introduced healthcare reform which extended health coverage to those who did not have it. By law, under Obamacare, all Americans must have health insurance. This is either paid for by themselves, their employer or, if they couldn't afford it, the state. **(3 marks KU)** Since the introduction of the Affordable Care Act, over 20 million people are estimated to have gained healthcare coverage showing the policy has had some success in tackling health issues in the USA. **(1 mark KU, 1 mark evaluation)** **Total 5 marks — 4 marks KU, 1 mark evaluation.** **World power: China** **Possible approach to answering this question:** **Response — China** Since the 1990s China has lifted more people out of poverty than any other country in the world due to economic reforms, government subsidies and increased pensions. **(1 mark KU)** China has also tackled urban poverty by offering government subsidies to bring minimum average incomes in urban areas up to $700. **(1 mark KU)** However, income and wealth inequality continues to be a huge problem with China having a high Gini coefficient of 0·46. **(1 mark analysis)** **Total 3 marks — 2 marks KU, 1 mark analysis.** **World power: South Africa** **Possible approach to answering this question:** **Response — South Africa** South Africa's National Development Plan has been created with the aim of eradicating extreme poverty and reducing South Africa's Gini coefficient from 0·7 to 0·6 by 2030. **(1 mark KU)** By 2017 the percentage living in the lowest poverty group had not changed since the NDP was introduced; however, South Africa's Gini coefficient had dropped to 0·62 showing that they are making some progress in tackling socio-economic inequality. **(1 mark KU, 1 mark evaluation)** **Total 3 marks — 2 marks KU, 1 mark evaluation.**

Question		General Marking Principles	Max marks	Specific Marking Instructions for this question
3.	(c)	Award an analysis mark where candidates use their knowledge and understanding or a source to identify relevant components (for example, of an idea, theory, argument) and clearly show at least one of the following: • links between different components • links between component(s) and the whole • links between component(s) and related concepts • similarities and contradictions • consistency and inconsistency • different views or interpretations • possible consequences or implications • the relative importance of components • understanding of underlying order or structure. Award up to **8 marks** for KU (description, explanation and exemplification) and up to **4 marks** for analytical comments. Award up to **6 marks** per point. Where candidates make more analytical points than are required to gain the maximum allocation of marks, award these as knowledge and understanding marks provided they meet the criteria for this.	12	Candidates can gain marks in a number of ways **up to a maximum of 12 marks.** Award marks where candidates refer to aspects of the following: • the nature of the issue • international organisations involved such as the United Nations organisations: World Trade Organisation, World Food Programme; Red Cross, Médecines Sans Frontières, European Union, NATO, SEATO • an analysis of the successes and/or shortcomings of the actions of these organisations and the reasons for these successes and/or failures. *Any other valid point that meets the criteria described in the general marking instructions for this type of question.* **World issue: Poverty in Africa** **Possible approach to answering this question:** **Response — Poverty in Africa** Poverty in Africa is often caused by ill health. One of the most serious diseases in Africa is malaria which affects millions of Africans, killing hundreds of thousands every year. **(1 mark KU)** People who are ill cannot work and so they and their families fall deeper into poverty. **(1 mark analysis)** The World Health Organization (WHO), which is part of the United Nations, is responsible for improving health around the world. The WHO has attempted to tackle malaria by providing drugs to treat people in poor areas. It has also provided millions of mosquito nets sprayed with insecticide to protect people when they are sleeping or praying. **(2 marks KU)** This is an effective way of controlling the mosquitoes which spread the disease and has resulted in many saved lives. However, the WHO's response to malaria is still considered inadequate by many as each of these nets only costs a few pounds yet one African child dies every 60 seconds as a result of malaria. **(1 mark analysis)** **Total 5 marks — 3 marks KU, 2 marks analysis.** **World issue: Conflict** **Possible approach to answering this question:** **Response — Conflict** During recent civil wars many people have become refugees as their homes have been destroyed by armed men. They now live in poverty as a result. **(1 mark KU)** **Total — 1 mark KU.** **World issue: AIDS** **Possible approach to answering this question:** **Response — AIDS** Many children in countries like Botswana have been left orphaned by AIDS. This has denied them an education and resulted in a lifetime of poverty. **(1 mark KU)** Their health is also affected as they are unable to afford what little healthcare is available. **(1 mark KU)** **Total — 2 marks KU.**

Question		General Marking Principles	Max marks	Specific Marking Instructions for this question
3.	(d)	Evaluation involves making judgements based on criteria, drawing conclusions on the extent to which a view is supported by the evidence; counter-arguments including possible alternative interpretations; the overall impact/ significance of the factors when taken together; the relative importance of factors in relation to the context. Award up to **8 marks** for KU (description, explanation and exemplification) and up to **4 marks** for evaluative comments. Award up to **6 marks** per point. Where a candidate makes more evaluative points than are required to gain the maximum allocation of marks, award these as knowledge and understanding marks provided they meet the criteria for this.	12	Candidates can gain marks in a number of ways **up to a maximum of 12 marks.** Award marks where candidates refer to: • the nature of the issue • impact on individuals, families and communities such as poverty, ill health and lower educational attainment • an evaluation of the relative severity of the impact of the issue. *Any other valid point that meets the criteria described in the general marking instructions for this kind type of question.* **World issue: Israeli/Palestinian conflict** **Possible approaches to answering this question:** **Response 1** The Israeli-Palestinian conflict has been going on for a long time. The conflict involves both sides recognising each other as a country and agreeing on which territories, for example Jerusalem, should belong to Israel or to Palestine. **(1 mark KU)** **Total — 1 mark KU.** **Response 2** The Israeli-Palestinian conflict has been going on for a long time. The conflict involves both sides recognising each other as a country and agreeing on which territories, for example Jerusalem, should belong to Israel or to Palestine. The conflict has resulted in around 16,000 people being killed, the majority of these are Palestinians. **(2 marks KU)** The Israeli economy fails to attract foreign investment due to this conflict which seriously hinders economic growth and leads to a much lower standard of living for its people. However, this problem is far more severe for the Palestinians who live in the Gaza Strip who are often forced to rely on foreign aid for survival. **(1 mark KU, 2 marks evaluation)** **Total 5 marks — 3 marks KU, 2 marks evaluation.** **Response 3** The areas known as the West Bank and the Gaza Strip are the two most disputed areas in the conflict. The Palestinians refer to this as Occupied Palestinian Territory whereas the Israelis say these are disputed territories as no one owned them when Israel captured them in 1967. **(2 marks KU)** The Gaza Strip which is only 25 km long has very high levels of poverty and unemployment. **(1 mark evaluation)** Israel blockaded the Gaza Strip in 2007 in order to curb the influence of the political group Hamas. Israel maintains the blockade has at no point caused a humanitarian crisis but aid agencies have criticised the conditions people have had to live in, in particular water supplies and toilet conditions. **(1 mark KU, 1 mark evaluation)** It is clear that innocent people are suffering in these two areas. As well as many violent deaths, health and education services are badly hampered leading to a great deal of avoidable suffering and an inability to create prosperity through investment and growth. **(1 mark KU, 1 mark evaluation)** **Total 7 marks — 4 marks KU, 3 marks evaluation.**

General marking principles for Higher Modern Studies Paper 2 (from 2019)

Marking principles for each question type

For each of the question types the following provides an overview of marking principles.

The information handling questions used in this paper are:

- to what extent is it accurate to state that ... **10 marks**
- what conclusions can be drawn ... **10 marks**
- to what extent are sources ... reliable **8 marks**

Objectivity questions (10 marks)

- Award up to **3 marks** for a single developed point depending on the use of the evidence in the sources and the quality of the analysis or evaluation.
- Award marks where candidates synthesise information both within and between sources.
- For **full marks** candidates must refer to all sources in their answer.
- Candidates must also make an overall judgement as to the extent of the accuracy of the given statement. Award a **maximum of 8 marks** if no overall judgement is made on extent of accuracy of the statement.

Conclusions questions (10 marks)

- Award up to **3 marks** for a single developed point depending on the use of the evidence in the sources and the quality of the analysis or evaluation.
- Award marks where candidates synthesise information both within and between sources.
- For **full marks** candidates must refer to all sources in their answer.
- Candidates are required to make an overall conclusion about the issue in the question. Award a **maximum of 8 marks** if candidates do not provide an overall conclusion.

Reliability questions (8 marks)

- Award up to **2 marks** for a single developed point depending on the use of the evidence in the sources and the quality of the analysis and/or evaluation.
- For **full marks** candidates must refer to all sources in their answer.
- Candidates must also make a judgement based on the evidence on the most reliable source. Award a **maximum of 6 marks** if candidates do not provide an overall judgement.
- Award a maximum of **3 marks** if only one factor is considered, for example, date, bias, sample size, provenance.

Higher Modern Studies marking grid for 10 mark source based (objectivity/conclusions) questions

<table>
<tr><th></th><th>1 mark</th><th>2 marks</th><th>3 marks</th><th>4 marks</th><th>5 marks</th><th>6 marks</th><th>7 marks</th><th>8 marks</th></tr>
<tr><td>Use of sources of evidence.
Award up to 8 marks.</td><td>Candidate uses one relevant piece of evidence from one source relating to one aspect of the issue.</td><td>Candidate links two distinct pieces of evidence relating to one aspect of the issue which may be from within a single source or between sources.</td><td>Candidate synthesises two distinct pieces of evidence relating to one aspect of the issue which may be from within a single source or between sources, and gives an evaluative comment.</td><td>In addition the candidate addresses a second aspect of the issue with reference to one relevant piece of evidence.</td><td>In addition the candidate addresses a second aspect of the issue with reference to linked evidence.</td><td>In addition the candidate addresses a second aspect of the issue is addressed with reference to synthesised evidence including an evaluative comment.</td><td>In addition the candidate addresses a third aspect of the issue with reference to one relevant piece of evidence.</td><td>In addition the candidate addresses a third aspect of the issue with reference to linked evidence
OR
synthesised evidence including an evaluative comment.</td></tr>
<tr><td>Objectivity
Candidate presents an analysis of the accuracy/ selectivity/ objectivity of a given view against the evidence.
Award up to 2 marks.</td><td>Candidate provides an objective assessment of a given view, based on evidence presented from the sources.</td><td>Candidate provides a detailed objective assessment of a given view, based on evidence presented from the sources.</td><td colspan="6" rowspan="2">1. For full marks candidates must refer to all sources in their answer. Award a maximum of 6 marks if all sources are not used.
2. Objectivity questions.
• Award up to 8 marks for an accurate evaluation of the given view using evidence.
• Award up to 2 marks for an overall judgement as to the extent of accuracy and/or objectivity of the view.
3. Conclusions questions.
For full marks candidates must make evaluative comments or judgement(s) or draw a conclusion about each of the points given in the question. Award a further 2 marks for an overall conclusion.</td></tr>
<tr><td>Conclusion
Candidate presents an overall evaluative comment(s) derived from a judgement of the evidence.
Award up to 2 marks.</td><td>Candidate presents an overall conclusion that is clear and supported by evidence from the sources.</td><td>Candidate presents an overall conclusion that is insightful and supported by detailed evidence from the sources.</td></tr>
</table>

Higher Modern Studies marking grid for 8 mark source based (reliability) questions

	1 mark	2 marks	3 marks	4 marks	5 marks	6 marks
Use of sources of evidence. Award up to **6 marks**.	Candidate uses one relevant piece of evidence accurately to explain the reliability of one source.	Candidate uses one relevant piece of evidence accurately to explain in detail the reliability of one source. **OR** Candidate uses two distinct pieces of evidence accurately to explain the reliability of one source.	In addition, the candidate uses one relevant piece of evidence accurately to explain the reliability of a second source.	In addition, the candidate uses one relevant piece of evidence accurately to explain in detail the reliability of a second source. **OR** Candidate uses two distinct pieces of evidence accurately to explain the reliability of a second source.	In addition, the candidate uses one relevant piece of evidence accurately to explain the reliability of a third source.	In addition, the candidate uses one relevant piece of evidence accurately to explain in detail the reliability of a third source. **OR** Candidate uses two distinct pieces of evidence accurately to explain the reliability of a third source.
Reliability Candidate presents an overall evaluative comment(s) on which source is the most reliable, derived from a judgement of the evidence. Award up to **2 marks**.	Candidate presents an overall conclusion on the most reliable source that is clear and supported by evidence from the sources.	Candidate presents an overall conclusion on the most reliable source that is insightful and supported by detailed evidence from all the sources.	1. For **full marks** candidates **must** refer to all sources in their answer. Award a maximum of **5 marks** if all sources are not used. Award a maximum of **3 marks** if only one factor is considered, for example, date, bias, sample size, provenance. 2. Award up to **6 marks** for an accurate evaluation of source reliability. Award a further **2 marks** for an overall judgement on the most reliable source.			

Conclusions question

<table>
<tr><th colspan="2">Question</th><th>General Marking Instructions</th><th>Max marks</th><th>Specific Marking Instructions for this question</th></tr>
<tr><td>1.</td><td></td><td>Candidates interpret and/or evaluate complex sources in order to reach conclusions.

In order to gain marks candidates must show evidence which explains the conclusions reached.
• Award up to 3 marks where candidates use evidence appropriately, depending on the quality of the explanation and the synthesis of the evidence to reach any one conclusion.
• For full marks candidates must refer to all sources in their answer.
• For full marks candidates must reach conclusions about each of the points given and make an overall conclusion on the issue.</td><td>10</td><td>Candidates can gain marks in a number of ways up to a maximum of 10 marks.

Possible approaches to answering this question:

The influence of poverty and social deprivation on voting behaviour.

Response 1
One conclusion is that a person's level of wealth can influence how they vote.

Total — 0 marks (valid conclusion but no evidence).

Response 2
Source A suggests that the more wealthy a person is the more likely they are to vote No. This is backed up by Source B which shows that those in social group ABC1 were more likely to vote No (57%) whereas those in C2DE were more likely to vote Yes (52%). This shows that a person's level of wealth influenced the way they voted with No voters having more wealth.

Total — 2 marks (synthesis across Sources A and B with conclusion).

Response 3
Source A states that the regions with higher levels of poverty were more likely to vote Yes. This is supported by Source A and Source C. In areas such as Glasgow and Dundee with high levels of unemployment, they were more likely to vote Yes. Moreover, in regions such as Aberdeen City and East Renfrewshire they had low unemployment levels of 1·4% and also had large No majorities of 58·6% and 63·2%, which was the highest No majority in the table. This shows that there is a link between levels of poverty and deprivation and how people voted, that is, lower poverty levels meant a lower Yes vote.

Total — 3 marks (complex synthesis between all three sources, and a conclusion).

The influence of age on voting behaviour.

Response 4
Source B shows that nearly three-quarters of voters aged 65 plus voted No. However, there were more Yes voters in the age brackets 16–24, 25–34, 35–44 and 45–54 but the margin was much narrower. This shows that age was a factor particularly within older voters and encouraged them to vote No.

Total — 2 marks (synthesis of information within Source B).

The link between turnout and regional voting.

Response 5
Turnout was generally lowest in regions that voted Yes.

Total — 0 marks (valid conclusion but no evidence).

Response 6
Both of the areas with lowest turnout voted Yes — Glasgow and Dundee. Source A shows 53·5% voted Yes in Glasgow, based on a turnout of 75%.

Total — 1 mark (valid conclusion with supporting evidence from Source A).

Response 7
The regions with the highest turnout were most likely to vote No, for example East Dunbartonshire had the highest turnout at 91% with almost two-thirds of voters voting No. Their turnout was a full 16% higher than Glasgow which had the lowest figure at 75%. In Glasgow, 46·5% of voters voted No which was approximately 16% less than in East Dunbartonshire. This pattern is repeated in East Renfrewshire which had the second highest turnout and in Dundee which had the second lowest turnout.

Total — 3 marks (valid conclusion with synthesis of evidence across Sources A and C and evaluation).</td></tr>
</table>

Question		General Marking Instructions	Max marks	Specific Marking Instructions for this question
1.		(continued)		**Possible overall conclusion about the most important factors influencing the outcome of the Scottish independence referendum.** **Response 8** The overall conclusion is that poverty levels were the most significant in influencing the outcome. Those regions that voted Yes – Glasgow, Dundee, North Lanarkshire and West Dunbartonshire – had the highest levels of child poverty. **Total – 2 marks (valid conclusion with evidence from Sources A and C).** **Response 9** Although several factors were important in deciding the outcome, such as age and deprivation, these are all less important than gender. Women voted decisively for the No side. This 58% No vote swung the result that way. The male No vote was only 53%. It is clear that the No majority among women was vital in creating the No decision. **Total – 2 marks (valid conclusion with evidence from Source B and evaluative comment).** **Response 10** Social class was important in deciding the result. **Total – 0 marks (valid conclusion but no evidence).** *Any other valid point that meets the criteria described in the general marking principles for this type of question.* **Do not award marks for a valid conclusion which is not supported with relevant source evidence.**

Objectivity question

Question		General Marking Instructions	Max marks	Specific Marking Instructions for this question
2.		Candidates interpret and/or evaluate complex sources of information, detecting and explaining the extent of objectivity. In order to gain marks candidates must show evidence which supports the extent of accuracy in a given viewpoint. • Award up to **3 marks** where candidates use evidence appropriately, depending on the quality of the explanation and the synthesis of the evidence, for any one explanation of the extent of objectivity. • For **full marks** candidates must refer to all sources in their answer. • For **full marks** candidates must make an overall judgement as to the extent of the accuracy of the given statement.	10	Candidates can gain marks in a number of ways **up to a maximum of 10 marks.** **Evidence that supports the view: 'Russia effectively protects the rights of its citizens'.** **Examples of the types of evidence that support the view include:** • there has been an extension of jury trials across the country (Source C) • the death penalty has been suspended (Source C) • no executions since 1996 (Source A) • fewer complaints – drop from 58,000 to 24,000 in two years (Source C) • right of protest is protected by Russian law (Source C) • campaign groups had the freedom to challenge the law in the courts (Source A) • better rights than China or Saudi Arabia (Source B). **Possible approach to answering this question:** **Response 1** The rights of Russians are well protected as in Source A campaign groups could take the government to court, which is an important right. This is supported by Source C which states that the right to protest is protected by Russian law and that registering as a foreign agent did not affect this right. **Total – 2 marks (evidence linked from two sources).**

Question		General Marking Instructions	Max marks	Specific Marking Instructions for this question
2.		(continued)		**Evidence that opposes the view: 'Russia effectively protects the rights of its citizens'.** **Examples of the types of evidence that support the view include:** • groups forced to register as foreign agents which is seen as 'traitor' by Russian people (Source A) • media campaign to discredit groups (Source A) • wide definition means a large number of campaign groups can be included (Source A) • leaders prosecuted and groups with no option but to disband (Source A) • court decision supports government, many complain about courts (Source A, Source C) • Russia compares badly to other major countries in Political Rights Index (PRI) meaning, for example, poor freedom of speech, participation (Source B backed up by information from Source A) • Russia rating on the PRI (Source B). **Possible approach to answering this question:** **Response 2** The rights of Russians are not effectively protected by the government as Russia's rating on the Political Rights Index (Source B) is the second lowest it could be. It has also been in decline from 3 to 6 in recent years. This shows that the right to participate and freedom of speech are not adequately protected. This is supported by Source A which shows that anyone campaigning for improvements has effectively been discredited as a foreign spy by the government. The right to protest may be protected by Russian law (Source C) but this won't be effective if the public are against 'foreign agents'. **Total — 3 marks (relevant evidence from all three sources with evaluative comment).** For **full marks**, candidates **must** make an overall judgement as to the extent of the accuracy of the given statement. **Examples of possible overall judgements:** • on the whole, the evidence suggests that Russia does not protect the rights of its citizens **(0 marks)** • the statement is largely untrue as the government has made it very difficult for any campaign groups to operate. This means that opposition to their policies is being silenced. Although jury trials are more widespread and there have been no executions since 1996, basic political rights are being denied. The Political Rights Index supports this conclusion as Russia's rating is declining over time and is only better than China and Saudi Arabia **(2 marks)** • Russia are doing well with human rights as the EU praised them for not executing anyone since 1996 **(1 mark)** • the statement is true to a certain extent, as there have been fewer complaints recently but they rank poorly on the Political Rights Index **(1 mark)** • the statement is true to a certain extent. **(0 marks)**

Reliability question

Question		General Marking Instructions	Max marks	Specific Marking Instructions for this question
3.		Candidates interpret and/or evaluate three complex sources of information, evaluating and explaining the extent of reliability. In order to gain marks candidates must show evidence which supports the evaluations reached. • Award up to **2 marks** where candidates use evidence appropriately, depending on the quality of the explanation and the synthesis of the evidence, for any one explanation of the extent of reliability. • For **full marks** candidates must refer to all sources in their answer. • For **full marks** candidates must make an overall conclusion on the most reliable source of information.	8	Candidates can gain marks in a number of ways **up to a maximum of 8 marks.** **Source A** **Response 1** Source A is not reliable. **Total — 0 marks (no evidence or explanation provided).** **Response 2** Source A is not reliable as it is an interview with a terrorist and only gives one person's perspective of the issue. **Total — 1 mark (straightforward evidence provided).** **Response 3** Source A is reliable and trustworthy to a certain extent. It has been published by a UK newspaper, the Independent, and although it will be biased, their journalist – in this case Shebab Khan, the author – should have followed journalistic ethics and standards when researching and writing this piece. **Total — 2 marks (detailed evidence provided).** **Source B** **Response 4** Source B is trustworthy as it is published by Ipsos Mori, a highly respected and professional polling organisation used by many media outlets. The sample of people questioned is representative, meaning it reflects the diversity of the population. **Total — 2 marks (detailed evidence provided).** **Source C** **Response 5** Although Source C is from a respected news organisation, Channel 4, which has high trust ratings among UK sources of news, this was published in 2009 which reduces the article's reliability as events will have changed since then and it will not contain the most up-to-date information. Therefore Source C's reliability is questionable. **Total — 2 marks (detailed evidence provided).** **Examples of an overall conclusion on the most reliable source of information:** **Response 6** Source A is the most reliable source as it is the most up to date having been published on 30 January 2016. **Total — 1 mark (overall conclusion supported by evidence from one source).** **Response 7** Source B is the most reliable source as the survey was carried out in January 2016 and is more up to date than Source C which was published in 2009. Source B is also likely to be more objective than Source A which is from a newspaper, and likely to be biased. **Total — 2 marks (overall conclusion supported by detailed evidence from all sources)** For **full marks**, candidates **must** make an overall judgement on the most reliable source.

HIGHER MODERN STUDIES 2019

General marking principles for Higher Modern Studies Paper 1

Marking principles for each question type

For each of the question types the following provides an overview of marking principles.

The extended-response questions used in this paper are

- discuss ... **20 marks**
- to what extent ... **20 marks**
- evaluate ... **12 marks**
- analyse ... **12 marks**

Extended response (12 or 20 marks)

For 12 mark questions, award up to **8 marks** for knowledge and understanding (description, explanation and exemplification). Award the remaining marks for the demonstration of higher-order skills of analysis **or** evaluation. Where a candidate makes more analytical/ evaluative points than are required to gain the **maximum allocation of 4 marks**, award as knowledge and understanding marks provided they meet the criteria for this.

For 20 mark questions, award **up to 8 marks** for knowledge and understanding (description, explanation and exemplification). Award the remaining marks for the demonstration of higher-order skills of analysis **and** evaluation **and** structured argument. Where a candidate makes more analytical/evaluative points than are required to gain the **maximum allocation of 6 marks**, award as knowledge and understanding marks provided they meet the criteria for this.

In Section 1 — Democracy in Scotland and the United Kingdom and Section 2 — Social Issues in the United Kingdom, award marks where candidates' responses refer to Scotland only, to the United Kingdom only, or to both Scotland and the United Kingdom.

- **Discuss** questions
  Candidates communicate ideas and information on the issue in the statement. Candidates gain marks for analysing and evaluating different views of the statement or viewpoint.
- **To what extent** questions
  Candidates gain marks for analysing the issue in the question and coming to a conclusion or conclusions which involve an evaluative judgement, which is likely to be quantitative in nature.
- **Evaluate** questions
  Candidates gain marks for making a judgement based on criteria; for determining the value of something.
- **Analyse** questions
  Candidates gain marks for identifying parts of an issue, the relationship between these parts and their relationships with the whole; and for drawing out and relating implications.

Higher Modern Studies marking grid for 20 mark questions (KU = 8 marks; analysis/evaluation = 12 marks)

	1 mark	2 marks	3 marks	4 marks	5–6 marks
Range of relevant knowledge Accurate, relevant, up to date	One relevant aspect of the issue given with some description.	Two relevant aspects of the issue given with some description **or** one relevant aspect covered with detailed and accurate description.	One relevant aspect of the issue with detailed and accurate description **and** one relevant aspect with some description.	At least two relevant aspects with detailed and accurate descriptions which should include the key aspects of the issue.	
Quality of explanation/ exemplification of the issue Award up to the **maximum of 8 marks** available for KU.	Some explanation of one aspect of the issue **or** relevant exemplification.	Some explanation of two relevant aspects of the issue **or** detailed explanation of one aspect of the question which may include relevant exemplification.	Detailed explanation of one relevant aspect of the issue with relevant exemplification **and** some explanation of one aspect of the question.	Full explanation of at least two aspects, which relate closely to the key aspects of the question **and** extended, relevant, accurate and up-to-date exemplification.	
Analysis Comments that identify relationships/implications explore different views or establish consequences and implications. Award up to **6 marks.***	One relevant and accurate analytical comment.	One relevant and accurate analytical comment that is justified **or** exemplified **or** two different relevant and accurate analytical comments.	One developed relevant and accurate analytical comment that is justified **and** exemplified; this should relate closely to a key aspect of the question.	One extended, accurate and justified analytical comment of an insightful nature which relates closely to the key aspects of the question and is exemplified.	At least two developed relevant and accurate analytical comments that are justified **and** exemplified. These should relate closely to the question and may be linked for **6 marks.**

	1 mark	2 marks	3 marks	4 marks	5–6 marks
Structure Develops a consistent and clear line of argument. Award up to **2 marks.**	Clear structure that addresses the issue identified in the question.	Structure that clarifies the issue, presents evidence and develops a clear and consistent line or argument.			
Conclusions Evaluative comments which make a judgement(s) and or reach a conclusion(s) which address the key issues in the question. Award up to **4 marks.***	One conclusion that addresses a key issue in the question.	One extended and balanced conclusion that addresses a key issue in the question **or** two conclusions that address key issues in the question.	One extended and balanced conclusion that is justified and directly addresses the key issue(s) in the question **or** two balanced conclusions that address the key issues in the question, one of which is extended.	One extended and balanced insightful conclusion that is justified and directly addresses the central aspects of the question **and** which considers a range of viewpoints.	

*Where a candidate makes more analytical and/or evaluative points required to gain the maximum allocation of marks, award these as knowledge and understanding marks, provided they meet the criteria for this.

Note: answers to **20 mark** questions should demonstrate at least two relevant aspects of knowledge and provide detailed analysis and evaluation.

For **full marks** in the KU aspect of the question (8/8), a response **must** include a range of points, have detailed explanation, and include a range of accurate exemplification.

Award **a maximum of 6 marks** (from 8 for KU) if there is no exemplification.

For **full marks** (20/20), a response **must** be structured, include a range of points, have detailed explanation, include a range of accurate and relevant exemplification and contain extended analysis and evaluation.

Higher Modern Studies marking grid for 12 mark questions (KU = 8 marks; analysis/evaluation = 4 marks)

	1 mark	2 marks	3 marks	4 marks
Range of relevant knowledge Accurate, relevant, uptodate.	One relevant aspect of the issue given with some description.	Two relevant aspects of the issue given with some description **or** one relevant aspect covered with detailed and accurate description.	One relevant aspect of the issue with detailed and accurate description **and** one relevant aspect with some description.	At least two relevant aspects with detailed and accurate descriptions which should include the key aspects of the issue.
Quality of explanation/ exemplification of the issue Award up to the **maximum of 8 marks** available for KU.	Some explanation of one aspect of the issue **or** relevant exemplification.	Some explanation of two relevant aspects of the issue **or** detailed explanation of one aspect of the question which may include relevant exemplification.	Detailed explanation of one relevant aspect of the issue with relevant exemplification **and** some explanation of one aspect of the question.	Full explanation of at least two aspects, which relate closely to the key aspects of the question **and** extended, relevant, accurate and upto-date exemplification.
Analysis/evaluation Comments that identify relationships, implications and make judgements Award up to **4 marks.***	One relevant and accurate analytical or evaluative comment.	One relevant and accurate analytical or evaluative comment that is justified **or** exemplified **or** two different relevant and accurate analytical/evaluative comments.	One developed relevant and accurate analytical or evaluative comment that is justified **and** exemplified; this should relate closely to a key aspect of the question.	One extended, accurate and justified analytical or evaluative comment of an insightful nature which relates closely to the key aspects of the question and is exemplified.

* Where a candidate makes more analytical/evaluative points than are required to gain the maximum allocation of marks, award these as knowledge and understanding marks, provided they meet the criteria for this.

Note: answers to **12 mark** questions should demonstrate at least two relevant aspects of knowledge.

For **full marks** in the KU aspect of the question (8/8), a response **must** include a range of points, have detailed explanation and include a range of accurate exemplification.

Award **a maximum of 6 marks** (from 8 for KU) if there is no accurate or relevant exemplification.

For **full marks** (12/12), a response **must** include a range of points, have detailed explanation, include a range of accurate and relevant exemplification and analysis or evaluation.

Section 1 – Democracy in Scotland and the United Kingdom

Question		General marking instructions	Max mark	Specific marking instructions for this question
1.	(a)	Award an analysis mark where candidates use their knowledge and understanding or a source to identify relevant components (for example, of an idea, theory, argument) and clearly show at least one of the following: • links between different components • links between component(s) and the whole • links between component(s) and related concepts • similarities and contradictions • consistency and inconsistency • different views or interpretations • possible consequences or implications • the relative importance of components • understanding of underlying order or structure. Evaluation involves making judgements based on criteria, drawing conclusions on the extent to which a view is supported by the evidence; counter-arguments including possible alternative interpretations; the overall impact or significance of the factors when taken together; the relative importance of factors in relation to the context. Award up to **8 marks** for KU (description, explanation and exemplification) and up to **12 marks** for analytical or evaluative comments. Award up to **6 marks** per point. Award up to **full marks** if candidates answer within a Scottish context only, a UK context only, or refer to both Scotland and the UK as appropriate. Where candidates make more analytical and/or evaluative points than are required to gain the maximum allocation of marks, award these as knowledge and understanding marks provided they meet the criteria for this.	20	Candidates can gain marks in a number of ways up to a **maximum of 20 marks.** Award marks where candidates refer to aspects of the following: • ongoing debate around alternative governance for Scotland • implications on Scotland and rest of UK of an alternative governance for Scotland. Candidates may refer to: • the ongoing debate around Independence and a second Independence Referendum • implications of Brexit vote on Scotland • devolution – the status quo • devolution max • 'the vow' • federalism • 'power grab' by Westminster during Brexit negotiations • the Calman Commission • the Smith Commission • constitutional implications of alternatives to the future governance of Scotland. *Any other valid point that meets the criteria described in the general marking instructions for this kind of question.* **Possible approaches to answering this question:** **Response 1** The Independence Referendum of 2014 was a victory for those that wished Scotland to remain part of the United Kingdom. Fifty-five % of Scottish voters said that they wanted to remain part of the UK. **(1 mark KU)** This shows that Scotland wishes to remain part of the UK and therefore this democratic vote should be respected. **(1 mark analysis)** **Total 2 marks – 1 mark KU, 1 mark analysis.** **Response 2** The Scottish Parliament currently has some powers in very important areas such as Health and Education. They have also been given some tax raising powers recently which means that Scottish people pay a higher rate of tax than people in the rest of the UK. **(1 mark KU)** Some groups such as the Labour Party, argue that by having these powers and being part of the UK, Scotland has the best of both worlds. **(1 mark KU)** They argue that there is no reason to change or become independent as Scotland has the benefit of extra powers and the protection of being part of the United Kingdom in, for example, Defence. **(1 mark analysis)** **Total 3 marks – 2 marks KU, 1 mark analysis.** **Response 3** Some people argue that decisions taken by Scotland are disregarded and overlooked by decisions taken in the rest of the UK. For example, some people argue that Scottish people were not listened to during the Brexit vote and that Scotland voted differently from large parts of the UK. **(1 mark analysis)** Sixty-two % of Scottish voters voted to remain part of the EU as opposed to 48% across the UK. **(1 mark KU)** Many argue that this is a democratic deficit which will see Scotland being forced to leave the EU against their will. They have argued that the best option for Scotland would be to be independent from the rest of the UK but still remain part of the EU. **(1 mark analysis)** This point of view is one that has been adopted by the SNP and has been described as 'feasible' by some MEPs in the European Parliament'. **(1 mark KU)** **Total 4 marks – 2 marks KU, 2 marks analysis.**

Question		General marking instructions	Max mark	Specific marking instructions for this question
1.	(a)	(continued)		**Response 4** Some people argue that Independence is the best way forward for Scotland. This means that Scotland would be fully responsible for all the decisions taken and powers used in Scotland. **(1 mark KU)** They argue that Westminster does not listen to the people of Scotland and often acts against their interests. In 2017, a motion brought by the SNP to the Scottish Parliament that called for a second Independence Referendum was passed by a majority of MSPs. However, the Prime Minister, Theresa May refused to back the proposals for a second referendum saying that, 'Now is not the time'. This highlights that even when the Scottish Parliament votes for something, Westminster can refuse or ignore the request. **(2 marks KU, 1 mark analysis)** This has led to a lot of anger from those in favour of Independence and is often used by them as their main argument as to why the current devolution settlement is unfair to Scotland. **(1 mark evaluation)** **Total 5 marks — 3 marks KU, 1 mark analysis, 1 mark evaluation.**
	(b)	Award an analysis mark where candidates use their knowledge and understanding or a source to identify relevant components (for example, of an idea, theory, argument) and clearly show at least one of the following: • links between different components • links between component(s) and the whole • links between component(s) and related concepts • similarities and contradictions • consistency and inconsistency • different views or interpretations • possible consequences or implications • the relative importance of components • understanding of underlying order or structure.	20	Candidates can gain marks in a number of ways up to a **maximum of 20 marks.** Award marks where candidates refer to aspects of the following: • the various ways that parliament can hold to account the work of government • the effectiveness or otherwise of parliament in holding to account the work of government. Candidates may refer to: **Scotland** • First Minister's Questions (FMQs) • work of committees • questions to individual ministers • voting • type of government can affect effectiveness — minority, majority or coalition — SNP having to rely on votes from other parties due to minority government • size of government majority • backbench rebellion • debates and motions • role and power of the whips • decision time. **UK** • Prime Minister's Questions (PMQs) • work of committees • questions to individual ministers • role of House of Lords as amending chamber • power of the whips • type of government — minority, majority and coalition 2017 Conservatives relying on DUP • size of government majority • backbench rebellion • Early Day Motions/Ten Minute Bills • voting • Salisbury Convention for policies in government manifesto.

Question		General marking instructions	Max mark	Specific marking instructions for this question
1.	(b)	(continued) Evaluation involves making judgements based on criteria, drawing conclusions on the extent to which a view is supported by the evidence; counter-arguments including possible alternative interpretations; the overall impact or significance of the factors when taken together; the relative importance of factors in relation to the context. Award up to **8 marks** for KU (description, explanation and exemplification) and up to **12 marks** for analytical or evaluative comments. Award up to **6 marks** per point. Award up to **full marks** if candidates answer within a Scottish context only, a UK context only, or refer to both Scotland and the UK as appropriate. Where candidates make more analytical and/or evaluative points than are required to gain the maximum allocation of marks, award these as knowledge and understanding marks provided they meet the criteria for this.		*Any other valid point that meets the criteria described in the general marking instructions for this kind of question.* **Possible approaches to answering this question:** **Response 1** There are many ways in which parliament can hold the government to account. Parliamentary representatives like MPs can question the Prime Minister at PMQs every Wednesday. **(1 mark KU)** **Total 1 mark — 1 mark KU.** **Response 2** There are many ways in which parliament can hold the government to account. Parliamentary representatives like MPs can question the Prime Minister at PMQs every Wednesday. **(1 mark KU)** PMQs is a good opportunity to hold the government to account. PMQs can be effective as it has the potential to embarrass the PM, the government and their policies. **(1 mark evaluation)** Labour MP David Lammy has asked many questions recently at PMQs particularly over the Windrush scandal which led to a review of policy relating to this. **(1 mark KU)** However, PMQs can be seen as being ineffective as many of the questions and PM responses are scripted and therefore much of the time for holding government to account is wasted. **(1 mark evaluation)** **Total 4 marks — 2 marks KU, 2 marks evaluation.** **Response 3** One way that parliament can hold the government to account is through individual backbenchers proposing new legislation which is then voted on by MSPs. **(1 mark KU)** The success of this often depends on the type of government in power. A minority government such as the current SNP government will struggle to defeat a Member's Bill particularly if all the opposition MSPs join forces and back the proposed piece of legislation. **(1 mark analysis)** This happened when Labour MSP James Kelly's Member's Bill was successful in overturning the SNP's Offensive Behaviour at Football Act. **(1 mark KU)** This shows that parliament can have some success against the government, particularly when the party in charge has a minority of the MSPs. **(1 mark evaluation)** **Total 4 marks — 2 marks KU, 1 mark analysis, 1 mark evaluation.** **Response 4** One of the main roles of parliament is to hold to account the work of government. Parliament can do this in many ways. They can ask questions of government ministers and they can take part in debates. They can also propose new laws themselves. Another good way is by proposing amendments to legislation put forward by the government. Parliament then votes on these amendments. **(1 mark KU)** In the UK, parliament includes members of the House of Lords. Recently, the House of Lords voted against the government over the terms of Britain leaving the EU. The House of Lords disagreed with the government and voted against the government's proposals. **(1 mark KU)** This shows that parliament has an important job and can hold to account the work of government. MPs also can be effective in holding to account the work of government such as forcing the government to seek changes to the 'Tampon Tax'. **(1 mark analysis)** However, the success of MPs in parliament is often dependent upon the type of government in power. A government with a minority of MPs, such as the Conservatives in 2017, is much more likely to be defeated and held to account by parliament more effectively than a government with a huge majority, such as Tony Blair's majority of 166 in 1997. **(1 mark KU, 1 mark analysis)** Theresa May's 2017 Conservative government has had to rely on the DUP to win some votes in parliament. This highlights how parliament can be very effective but is sometimes limited by the size and type of government. **(1 mark evaluation)** **Total 6 marks — 3 marks KU, 2 analysis, 1 mark evaluation.**

Question		General marking instructions	Max mark	Specific marking instructions for this question
1.	(c)	Award an analysis mark where candidates use their knowledge and understanding or a source to identify relevant components (for example, of an idea, theory, argument) and clearly show at least one of the following: • links between different components • links between component(s) and the whole • links between component(s) and related concepts • similarities and contradictions • consistency and inconsistency • different views or interpretations • possible consequences or implications • the relative importance of components • understanding of underlying order or structure. Evaluation involves making judgements based on criteria, drawing conclusions on the extent to which a view is supported by the evidence; counter-arguments including possible alternative interpretations; the overall impact or significance of the factors when taken together; the relative importance of factors in relation to the context. Award up to **8 marks** for KU (description, explanation and exemplification) and up to **12 marks** for analytical or evaluative comments. Award up to **6 marks** per point. Award up to **full marks** if candidates answer within a Scottish context only, a UK context only, or refer to both Scotland and the UK as appropriate. Where candidates make more analytical and/or evaluative points than are required to gain the maximum allocation of marks, award these as knowledge and understanding marks provided they meet the criteria for this.	20	Candidates can be credited in a number of ways up to a **maximum of 20 marks.** Award marks where candidates refer to aspects of the following: • types of pressure groups and the methods they use • effectiveness of pressure groups and the methods they use. Candidates may refer to: • types of pressure groups: insider and outsider groups, sectional and interest groups • success often dependent upon political leanings of party in power • types of methods used, for example, petitions (including e-petitions), marches, non-violent direct action, lobbying • individual backing of pressure group campaigns by MPs and MSPs • ways in which some pressure groups use the media to influence decision-making through public opinion • backing of MPs by trade unions and business organisations • use of social media and internet • role and influence of paid lobbyists within the House of Lords and the Commons. *Any other valid point that meets the criteria described in the general marking instructions for this kind of question.* **Possible approaches to answering this question:** **Response 1** Some groups outside of parliament are more effective than others in influencing governmental decision-making. For example, insider groups can be said to be more successful and effective in influencing government policy than outsider groups. **(1 mark evaluation)** Insider groups generally have strong links to the government and are often asked by the government for their opinion and ideas on areas that they are familiar with. **(1 mark KU)** **Total 2 marks — 1 mark KU, 1 mark evaluation.** **Response 2** The success of pressure groups often depends on the type of methods used and how they appear to the general public. Groups such as CND actively break the law through non-violent direct action which often leads to many members and supporters being arrested during events such as the Big Blockade at Faslane Naval Base. **(1 mark KU)** On the one hand, this generates a great deal of publicity for their cause and may increase the number of people supporting them. **(1 mark analysis)** However, their methods could alienate members of the public who don't think it is right to break the law to make a point. **(1 mark analysis)** **Total 3 marks — 1 mark KU, 2 marks analysis.** **Response 3** Some groups outside of parliament are more effective than others in influencing governmental decision-making. For example, insider groups can be said to be more successful and effective in influencing government policy than outsider groups. **(1 mark evaluation)** Insider groups generally have strong links to the government and are often asked by the government for their opinion and ideas on areas that they are familiar with. **(1 mark KU)** The success of insider lobby groups often depends on the political party in power, for example, a pro-business, pro-employer group such as the CBI are likely to have more success when a Conservative government is in power. **(1 mark KU, 1 mark analysis)** Likewise, a Labour government with Jeremy Corbyn as Prime Minister will be more likely to listen to pro trade union groups such as the Trades Union Congress or a union such as Unison. The effectiveness of these groups therefore will often depend upon the political leanings of which party is in power. **(1 mark KU, 1 mark analysis)** **Total 6 marks — 3 marks KU, 2 marks analysis, 1 mark evaluation.**

Section 2 – Social inequality

<table>
<tr><th colspan="2">Question</th><th>General marking instructions</th><th>Max mark</th><th>Specific marking instructions for this question</th></tr>
<tr><td>2.</td><td>(a)</td><td>Award an analysis mark where candidates use their knowledge and understanding or a source, to identify relevant components (for example, of an idea, theory, argument) and clearly show at least one of the following:
• links between different components
• links between component(s) and the whole
• links between component(s) and related concepts
• similarities and contradictions
• consistency and inconsistency
• different views or interpretations
• possible consequences or implications
• the relative importance of components
• understanding of underlying order or structure.

Award up to 8 marks for KU (description, explanation and exemplification) and up to 4 marks for analytical comments.

Award up to 6 marks per point.

Award up to full marks if candidates answer within a Scottish context only, a UK context only, or refer to both Scotland and the UK as appropriate.

Where candidates make more analytical points than are required to gain the maximum allocation of marks, award these as knowledge and understanding marks provided they meet the criteria for this.</td><td>12</td><td>Candidates can gain marks in a number of ways up to a maximum of 12 marks.

Award marks where candidates refer to aspects of the following:
• social inequality affecting the group
• economic inequality affecting the group.

Candidates may refer to
• young/old
• gender differences
• ethnicity
• social/economic status
• disability.

Any other point that meets the criteria described in the general marking instructions for this kind of question.

If a response considers more than one distinct group, it should only be credited for the one which attracts the highest mark.

Possible approaches to answering this question:

Response 1
People from minority ethnic backgrounds in the UK are paid 26% less on average than the majority white population. (1 mark KU)

Total 1 mark – 1 mark KU.

Response 2
People from minority ethnic backgrounds in the UK are paid 26% less on average than the majority white population. (1 mark KU) This can lead to a lifetime average difference of around £500,000. (1 mark KU) This is a clear income inequality and makes securing a mortgage more difficult meaning that many BAME workers live in poorer housing. (1 mark analysis)

Total 3 marks – 2 marks KU, 1 mark analysis.

Response 3
Despite decades of equal opportunities legislation, most recently the Equality Act (2010), the UK's Black and minority ethnic population still faces inequality. (1 mark KU) Lower levels of pay (26% lower on average than that of Whites) leads to a higher chance of living in poverty for example, according to the JRF, the BAME population has poverty rates around twice the level of those among the white population. (1 mark KU, 1 mark analysis) The BAME population is more likely to find employment in sectors of the economy with lower wages, such as the retail sector. (1 mark KU) This in turn contributes to lower educational attainment among some BAME communities. For example, males from the Black Caribbean community are most likely (18%) to leave school with no qualifications. (1 mark KU, 1 mark analysis)

Total 6 marks – 4 marks KU, 2 marks analysis.</td></tr>
</table>

Question		General marking instructions	Max mark	Specific marking instructions for this question
2.	(b)	Evaluation involves making judgements based on criteria, drawing conclusions on the extent to which a view is supported by the evidence; counter-arguments including possible alternative interpretations; the overall impact/ significance of the factors when taken together; the relative importance of factors in relation to the context. Award up to **8 marks** for KU (description, explanation and exemplification) and up to **4 marks** for analytical comments. Award up to **6 marks** per point. Award up to **full marks** if candidates answer within a Scottish context only, a UK context only, or refer to both Scotland and the UK as appropriate. Where candidates make more evaluative points than are required to gain the maximum allocation of marks, award these as knowledge and understanding marks provided they meet the criteria for this.	12	Candidates can gain marks in a number of ways up to a **maximum of 12 marks.** Award marks where candidates refer to aspects of the following: • government policies that tackle inequalities • successes/failures of policies. Candidates may refer to: • government policies designed to tackle income/wealth inequalities • government policies designed to tackle health inequalities • government policies designed to tackle housing inequalities • government policies designed to tackle education inequalities. *Any other valid point that meets the criteria described in the general marking instructions for this type of question.* **Possible approaches to answering this question:** **Response 1** In all sectors, low-paid and well-paid women still earn less than men. In part to tackle the gender pay gap the government introduced the National Minimum Wage in 1999. **(1 mark KU)** **Total 1 mark — 1 mark KU.** **Response 2** In all sectors, low-paid and well-paid women still earn less than men. In part to tackle the gender pay gap the government introduced the National Minimum Wage in 1999. **(1 mark KU)** The NMW helps women more than men due to the fact the NMW benefits 3 in 10 women and women make up 60% of all lowest paid employees. **(1 mark KU)** The NMW especially helps women who work in the 5 Cs — catering, cleaning, clerical, caring and cashier. **(1 mark KU)** This highlights that as women make up the majority of low-paid positions the NMW has been most beneficial in increasing their income. **(1 mark evaluation)** **Total 4 marks — 3 marks KU, 1 mark evaluation.** **Response 3** In all sectors, low-paid and well-paid women still earn less than men. In part to tackle the gender pay gap the government introduced the National Minimum Wage in 1999. **(1 mark KU)** The NMW helps women more than men due to the fact the NMW benefits 3 in 10 women and women make up 60% of all lowest paid employees. **(1 mark KU)** The NMW especially helps women who work in the 5 Cs — catering, cleaning, clerical, caring and cashier. **(1 mark KU)** This highlights that as women make up the majority of low-paid positions, the NMW has been most beneficial in increasing their income. **(1 mark evaluation)** However, many would argue that the NMW is unsuccessful as some people believe it raises unemployment by making workers too expensive to employ. Others argue the NMW is regarded as being too low, at only £8·21 for those over 25 (referred to as the National Living Wage). **(1 mark KU, 1 mark evaluation)** Therefore, this shows that government have been fairly successful but as there is still a gender pay gap, more must be done that the NMW alone won't fix. **(1 mark evaluation)** **Total 7 marks — 4 marks KU, 3 marks evaluation.** ***Note:*** *apply the* ***6 marks maximum*** *for response 3 as it only addresses one point (National Minimum Wage).*

<table>
<tr><th colspan="2">Question</th><th>General marking instructions</th><th>Max mark</th><th>Specific marking instructions for this question</th></tr>
<tr><td>2.</td><td>(c)</td><td>Award an analysis mark where candidates use their knowledge and understanding or a source, to identify relevant components (for example, of an idea, theory, argument) and clearly show at least one of the following:
• links between different components
• links between component(s) and the whole
• links between component(s) and related concepts
• similarities and contradictions
• consistency and inconsistency
• different views or interpretations
• possible consequences or implications
• the relative importance of components
• understanding of underlying order or structure.

Award up to 8 marks for KU (description, explanation and exemplification) and up to 4 marks for analytical comments.

Award up to 6 marks per point.

Award up to full marks if candidates answer within a Scottish context only, a UK context only, or refer to both Scotland and the UK as appropriate.

Where candidates make more analytical points than are required to gain the maximum allocation of marks, award these as knowledge and understanding marks provided they meet the criteria for this.</td><td>12</td><td>Candidates can gain marks in a number of ways up to a maximum of 12 marks.

Award marks where candidates refer to aspects of the following:
• types of crime
• effects of crime on the victim.

Candidates may refer to:
• range of types of crimes, for example violent and non-violent
• short and long-term effects of crime on the victim, for example physical, emotional, financial, psychological
• reference to official crime figures
• case studies and examples with reference to effects of different crimes.

Any other valid point that meets the criteria described in the general marking instructions for this type of question.

Possible approaches to answering this question:

Response 1
A person can suffer physical and mental consequences as a result of being a victim of crime. A victim can be left injured, disabled or scarred for life if they suffer a physical attack. (1 mark KU)

Total 1 mark — 1 mark KU.

Response 2
A person can suffer physical and mental consequences as a result of being a victim of crime. A victim can be left injured, disabled or scarred for life if they suffer a physical attack. (1 mark KU) This in turn can change a person's whole life as they may find it more difficult to get a job if they have an obvious scar, because of discrimination. (1 mark analysis)

Total 2 marks — 1 mark KU, 1 mark analysis.

Response 3
A person can suffer physical and mental consequences as a result of being a victim of crime. A victim can be left injured, disabled or scarred for life if they suffer a physical attack. (1 mark KU) This in turn can change a person's whole life as they may find it more difficult to get a job if they have an obvious scar, because of discrimination. (1 mark analysis) After being the victim of a violent assault the mental trauma can last months or years. The person may be reluctant to venture out and may find themselves suffering from mental illness such as depression and anxiety. (1 mark KU) A combination of unemployment and mental illness may often lead to a lower income and a greater chance of experiencing poverty. (1 mark analysis)

Total 4 marks — 2 marks KU, 2 marks analysis.</td></tr>
</table>

<table>
<tr><th colspan="2">Question</th><th>General marking instructions</th><th>Max mark</th><th>Specific marking instructions for this question</th></tr>
<tr><td>2.</td><td>(d)</td><td>Evaluation involves making judgements based on criteria, drawing conclusions on the extent to which a view is supported by the evidence; counter-arguments including possible alternative interpretations; the overall impact/ significance of the factors when taken together; the relative importance of factors in relation to the context.

Award up to 8 marks for KU (description, explanation and exemplification) and up to 4 marks for analytical comments.

Award up to 6 marks per point.

Award up to full marks if candidates answer within a Scottish context only, a UK context only, or refer to both Scotland and the UK as appropriate.

Where candidates make more evaluative points than are required to gain the maximum allocation of marks, award these as knowledge and understanding marks provided they meet the criteria for this.</td><td>12</td><td>Candidates can gain marks in a number of ways up to a maximum of 12 marks.

Award marks where candidates refer to aspects of the following:
• various methods of non-custodial responses
• success/failures of non-custodial responses.

Candidates may refer to:
• Community Payback Orders (CPOs)
• Restriction of Liberty Orders (RLOs)
• electronic tagging
• restorative justice
• Drug Treatment and Testing Orders (DTTOs)
• statistical evidence and official crime figures
• case studies and examples with reference to different crimes/ criminals.

Any other valid point that meets the criteria described in the general marking instructions for this type of question.

Possible approaches to answering this question:

Response 1
Community Payback Orders (CPOs) are targeted at those offenders who haven't committed particularly serious crimes. They aim to change the offender's behaviour towards their community and their attitude to go out and work. (1 mark KU)

Total 1 mark — 1 mark KU.

Response 2
Community Payback Orders (CPOs) are targeted at those offenders who haven't committed particularly serious crimes. They aim to change the offender's behaviour towards their community and their attitude to go out and work. (1 mark KU) CPOs consist of unpaid work, offender supervision as well as often consisting of mental health treatment, drug and alcohol therapy. (1 mark KU)

Total 2 marks — 2 marks KU.

Response 3
Community Payback Orders (CPOs) are targeted at those offenders who haven't committed particularly serious crimes. They aim to change the offender's behaviour towards their community and their attitude to go out and work. (1 mark KU) CPOs consist of unpaid work, offender supervision as well as often consisting of mental health treatment, drug and alcohol therapy. (1 mark KU) It has been proven that offenders who serve a CPO instead of a custodial sentence are four times less likely to end up in custody for future offences. This highlights a key success of CPOs in that they not only ensure the offenders are contributing something positive back into society, but they also ensure offenders are rehabilitated afterwards. (1 mark KU, 1 mark evaluation)

Total 4 marks — 3 marks KU, 1 mark evaluation.</td></tr>
</table>

Section 3 – International issues

Question		General marking instructions	Max mark	Specific marking instructions for this question
3.	(a)	Award an analysis mark where candidates use their knowledge and understanding or a source to identify relevant components (for example, of an idea, theory, argument) and clearly show at least one of the following: • links between different components • links between component(s) and the whole • links between component(s) and related concepts • similarities and contradictions • consistency and inconsistency • different views or interpretations • possible consequences or implications • the relative importance of components • understanding of underlying order or structure. Evaluation involves making judgements based on criteria, drawing conclusions on the extent to which a view is supported by the evidence; counter-arguments including possible alternative interpretations; the overall impact or significance of the factors when taken together; the relative importance of factors in relation to the context. Award up to **8 marks** for KU (description, explanation and exemplification) and up to **12 marks** for analytical or evaluative comments. Award up to **6 marks** per point. Where candidates make more analytical and/or evaluative points than are required to gain the maximum allocation of marks, award these as knowledge and understanding marks provided they meet the criteria for this.	20	Candidates can gain marks in a number of ways up to a **maximum of 20 marks.** Award marks where candidates refer to aspects of the following: • the political system of the world power studied • the relative powers of different political institutions. Candidates may refer to: • the role of political parties • executive authority held by the President/Prime Minister/Cabinet • authority held by main legislative bodies • judicial authority • relationship between the executive, legislative and judicial bodies • relationship between national, state, provincial and local governments. *Any other valid point that meets the criteria described in the general marking instructions for this type of question.* **Possible approaches to answering this question:** **World power: USA** The US political system was designed to separate executive, legislative and judicial powers to ensure that no one political institution was able to dominate decision-making. **(1 mark KU)** For example, the Congress proposes and ratifies legislation, but each bill must be signed by the President if it is to become law. **(1 mark KU)** **Total 2 marks – 2 marks KU.** **World power: China** **Response 1** The Chinese Constitution sets out a system that divides executive, legislative and judicial authority within the country to be held by the President, the National People's Congress and the Supreme People's Court. **(1 mark KU)** However, in reality each branch of government is controlled by the Communist Party of China (CPC) and it acts to rubber stamp its decisions. **(1 mark KU)** This shows that the CPC dominates all government decision-making to a significant extent and does not face scrutiny by other political institutions. **(1 mark evaluation)** **Total 3 marks – 2 marks KU, 1 mark evaluation.** **Response 2** Within China, legislative powers are held by the National People's Congress (NPC), which forms China's parliament. The NPC has the power to pass legislation and to appoint the President and ratify their nomination for the Premier. **(1 mark KU)** However, the NPC meets only once a year and 2119 of the 2980 members belong to the Communist Party. **(1 mark KU)** This means that the NPC has relatively little influence within China as it does not meet regularly enough to do more than just ratify legislation, and when it does meet the Communist Party of China (CPC) has a vast majority within it and can control decision-making. **(1 mark analysis)** Overall, it is clear that as a result of its dominance within the legislature the CPC is able to dominate government decision-making and that it faces little scrutiny. **(1 mark evaluation)** **Total 4 marks – 2 marks KU, 1 mark analysis, 1 mark evaluation.**

Question		General marking instructions	Max mark	Specific marking instructions for this question
3.	(a)	(continued)		**World power: South Africa** The President is elected to office by the National Assembly rather than directly by the public which shows that his ability to dominate decision-making is potentially limited due to his reliance on the Assembly. **(1 mark KU, 1 mark analysis)** However, former President Jacob Zuma managed to be re-elected to a second term in 2014 despite accusations in 2013 that he spent millions of rand of taxpayers' money on a swimming pool at his private home. **(1 mark KU)** His ability to hold onto power, despite facing political scandals, shows that the President's power is extensive and that he faces only weak scrutiny from the legislative. **(1 mark evaluation)** However, in reality the reason he was able to maintain his power in government is because he was the ANC party leader. The ANC dominates election results winning a majority of over 60% of the National Assembly. **(1 mark analysis)** When President Zuma attempted to extend his own rule by proposing his wife to be the new ANC leader in 2017 he was forced out by the ANC who elected Cyril Ramaphosa to be the new leader instead which forced Zuma to resign his Presidency in 2018. **(1 mark KU)** This shows that whilst decision-making in South Africa is dominated by the President, it is in reality the political institution of the ANC party that is able to dominate government decision-making as it chooses the President. **(1 mark evaluation)** **Total 7 marks — 3 marks KU, 2 marks analysis, 2 marks evaluation.** ***Note:*** *apply the* ***6 marks maximum*** *for South Africa response as it only addresses one point (powers of the President).*
	(b)	Award an analysis mark where candidates use their knowledge and understanding or a source to identify relevant components (for example, of an idea, theory, argument) and clearly show at least one of the following: • links between different components • links between component(s) and the whole • links between component(s) and related concepts • similarities and contradictions • consistency and inconsistency • different views or interpretations • possible consequences or implications • the relative importance of components • understanding of underlying order or structure.	20	Candidates can gain marks in a number of ways up to a **maximum of 20 marks.** Award marks where candidates refer to aspects of the following: • the political, economic, cultural and military influence • the extent of the influence. Candidates may refer to: **World power: China** • political influence — permanent membership of the UN Security Council with a veto over decisions — 'soft power' lobbying activities worldwide • economic influence — membership of the G20 — investment in Africa — trade influence — China is the second largest importer of goods and services • military influence — nuclear power — the People's Liberation Army is the largest military in the world — it has increased spend and been growing its military assets in recent years. **World power: South Africa** • political influence — membership and influence in the African Union — South Africa will sit on the UN Security Council in 2019 and has already sat on the council in 2007–2008 and 2011–2012 • economic influence — membership of the G20 — membership of BRICS and IBSA countries — second largest economy in Africa • military influence — South African National Defence Force — contributions to UN Peacekeeping missions on the continent, for example supporting MONUSCO in the DRC.

Question		General marking instructions	Max mark	Specific marking instructions for this question
3.	(b)	(continued) Evaluation involves making judgements based on criteria, drawing conclusions on the extent to which a view is supported by the evidence; counter-arguments including possible alternative interpretations; the overall impact or significance of the factors when taken together; the relative importance of factors in relation to the context. Award up to **8 marks** for KU (description, explanation and exemplification) and up to **12 marks** for analytical or evaluative comments. Award up to **6 marks** per point. Where candidates make more analytical and/or evaluative points than are required to gain the maximum allocation of marks, award these as knowledge and understanding marks provided they meet the criteria for this.		**World power: USA** • political influence – permanent membership of the UN Security Council with a veto over decisions – political influence worldwide – role in Middle East peace negotiations – role as a nuclear superpower and leading role in negotiating/policing nuclear disarmament – Obama's deal with Iran, Trump's potential role in negotiating North Korea disarmament • economic influence – membership of the G7 and G20 – economic power and influence over world trade • military influence – leading role in NATO – despite 'collective decision-making' the USA contributes 70% of budget – military power and involvement in global conflicts such as Syria and Libya and withdrawal from Afghanistan and Iraq – reference to USA as 'world policeman'. Any candidate who considers the cultural influence of a world power should be awarded **a maximum of six marks** for this section. *Any other valid point that meets the criteria described in the general marking instructions for this type of question.* **Possible approaches to answering this question:** **World power: China** China's People's Liberation Army is the largest military in the world which allows it to demonstrate a significant power through its large military displays and marches. **(1 mark KU)** China is also a nuclear power and one of the five official Nuclear Weapons States in the world. **(1 mark KU)** **Total 2 marks – 2 marks KU.** **World power: South Africa** South Africa's economy is still in development but its international economic influence is increasing. They are the only African member of the G20 which allows it to be involved in discussions on global economic policy. **(1 mark KU)** As the only African member it acts as a representative for the continent within the G20 and its influence therefore extends beyond its own borders. **(1 mark analysis)** South Africa's economy is the second largest in Africa and therefore has a significant regional influence on trade matters, however it struggles to compete with larger economies around the world such as the USA and China. **(1 mark analysis)** This means that whilst South Africa does have an international economic influence it is limited by nature to the African region or as a spokesperson for the region. **(1 mark evaluation)** **Total 4 marks – 1 mark KU, 2 marks analysis, 1 mark evaluation.**

<table>
<tr><th colspan="2">Question</th><th>General marking instructions</th><th>Max mark</th><th>Specific marking instructions for this question</th></tr>
<tr><td>3.</td><td>(b)</td><td>(continued)</td><td></td><td>World power: USA
The USA has a significant influence on the world due to its political power. America has a permanent membership of the UN Security Council which means it can both propose and veto UNSC resolutions. (1 mark KU) For example, the US proposed a resolution in 2017 to impose new sanctions on North Korea in response to their missile tests which was unanimously accepted. (1 mark KU) They can also veto resolutions and they can use this to pursue their own agenda. In 2017 the US used its veto to stop a resolution which would have called for them to withdraw Donald Trump's recognition of Jerusalem as Israel's capital. This shows that the US has a significant influence on international political decision-making as it is able to use its seat on the Security Council to further its own agenda. (1 mark KU, 1 mark analysis) However, it is not the only country to hold a veto and as a result the USA cannot force through a decision which shows a limitation to its influence. The USA has not been able to get a resolution passed that would respond to the use of chemical weapons in Syria because it has been vetoed by Russia. This shows that their political influence can be limited by other influential countries. (1 mark KU, 1 mark evaluation)
Total 6 marks — 4 marks KU, 1 mark analysis, 1 mark evaluation.</td></tr>
<tr><td></td><td>(c)</td><td>Award an analysis mark where candidates use their knowledge and understanding or a source to identify relevant components (for example, of an idea, theory, argument) and clearly show at least one of the following:
• links between different components
• links between component(s) and the whole
• links between component(s) and related concepts
• similarities and contradictions
• consistency and inconsistency
• different views or interpretations
• possible consequences or implications
• the relative importance of components
• understanding of underlying order or structure.</td><td>20</td><td>Candidates can gain marks in a number of ways up to a maximum of 20 marks.
Award marks where candidates refer to aspects of the following:
• the effects of a world issue
• to what extent do these effects have international influence.
World issue: Development in Africa
Candidates may refer to:
• impact of economic migrants on European countries and the wider world
• increase in terrorism and development of Boko Haram and IS activity across the globe
• health epidemics, for example Ebola and its spread to Europe
• cost of aid programmes to other countries and to international organisations such as the UN, WFP
• benefits to the developed world of African health professionals, e.g. brain drain
• changing demands on international charities, and changing public attitudes for example compassion fatigue
• debt owed to/written off by international banks.
Any other valid point that meets the criteria described in the general marking instructions for this type of question.
Possible approach to answering this question:
Response
There was a significant international programme of support to help prevent the recent Ebola epidemic spreading further which was both costly to the donor countries and potentially dangerous as aid workers could contract the disease. It is estimated that the USA, the UK and Germany spent $3·6 billion on this programme. (1 mark KU, 1 mark analysis) A poor health infrastructure in one country can have an international effect as it can cause problems within the region and across the wider world, for example the Scottish nurse who caught Ebola whilst working for a charity in Sierra Leone. (1 mark KU) This had a major impact on the UK because there was a public health scare which was very costly, impacting greatly on society. (1 mark evaluation)
Total 4 marks — 2 marks KU, 1 mark analysis, 1 mark evaluation.</td></tr>
</table>

<table>
<tr><th colspan="2">Question</th><th>General marking instructions</th><th>Max mark</th><th>Specific marking instructions for this question</th></tr>
<tr><td>3.</td><td>(c)</td><td>(continued)

Evaluation involves making judgements based on criteria, drawing conclusions on the extent to which a view is supported by the evidence; counter-arguments including possible alternative interpretations; the overall impact or significance of the factors when taken together; the relative importance of factors in relation to the context.

Award up to 8 marks for KU (description, explanation and exemplification) and up to 12 marks for analytical or evaluative comments.

Award up to 6 marks per point.

Where candidates make more analytical and/or evaluative points than are required to gain the maximum allocation of marks, award these as knowledge and understanding marks provided they meet the criteria for this.</td><td></td><td>World issue: Conflict

Candidates may refer to:
• the impact of refugees from conflict zones on neighbouring countries and the wider world
• impact of conflict on oil prices
• impact of terrorist groups outside the immediate conflict zone
• increase in overall political instability, for example resurgence of Cold War tensions over Syria.

Any other valid point that meets the criteria described in the general marking instructions for this type of question.

Possible approach to answering this question:

Response
The Syrian Civil War has now been ongoing since 2011 and has caused around 5 million people to flee Syria as refugees. (1 mark KU) This has created a crisis in neighbouring countries who have struggled to house the influx of refugees. Most of these refugees are now in Turkey, Lebanon, Jordan, Iraq and Egypt with 10% going further to Europe. (1 mark KU) The infrastructure in host countries is often not sufficient to manage the numbers of people now reliant on it which goes on to cause increased tensions between refugees and the host population increasing the chances of civil unrest. (1 mark analysis) A consequence of this unrest has been the mass movement of Syrian refugees towards the EU. This has resulted in a huge loss of life in the Mediterranean Sea and a humanitarian crisis in Southern Europe costing many billions of euros. This may also have been partly responsible for the rise of populist right-wing parties across much of Europe, for example AFD in Germany. (1 mark KU, 2 marks analysis)

Total 6 marks — 3 marks KU, 3 marks analysis.

World issue: International terrorism

Candidates may refer to:
• rise of ISIS has led to increased attacks around the world and an increase in instability
• increased security measures across the world
• increased threat to human rights across the world
• online propaganda and recruitment tactics used by groups such as ISIS
• worsening relationships in the Middle East between Saudi Arabia and Iran.

Any other valid point that meets the criteria described in the general marking instructions for this type of question.

Possible approach to answering this question:

Response
The UK government has tried to increase surveillance powers on social media as a result of attacks such as that on British Army soldier Lee Rigby. (1 mark KU) Many human rights groups have argued that this is an infringement on our right to privacy and as such should be abandoned. (1 mark analysis)

Total 2 marks — 1 mark KU, 1 mark analysis.</td></tr>
</table>

<table>
<tr><th colspan="2">Question</th><th>General marking instructions</th><th>Max mark</th><th>Specific marking instructions for this question</th></tr>
<tr><td>3.</td><td>(d)</td><td>Award an analysis mark where candidates use their knowledge and understanding or a source to identify relevant components (for example, of an idea, theory, argument) and clearly show at least one of the following:
• links between different components
• links between component(s) and the whole
• links between component(s) and related concepts
• similarities and contradictions
• consistency and inconsistency
• different views or interpretations
• possible consequences or implications
• the relative importance of components
• understanding of underlying order or structure.

Evaluation involves making judgements based on criteria, drawing conclusions on the extent to which a view is supported by the evidence; counter-arguments including possible alternative interpretations; the overall impact or significance of the factors when taken together; the relative importance of factors in relation to the context.

Award up to 8 marks for KU (description, explanation and exemplification) and up to 12 marks for analytical or evaluative comments.

Award up to 6 marks per point.

Where candidates make more analytical and/or evaluative points than are required to gain the maximum allocation of marks, award these as knowledge and understanding marks provided they meet the criteria for this.</td><td>20</td><td>Candidates can be credited in a number of ways up to a maximum of 20 marks.

Award marks where candidates refer to aspects of the following:
• the responses by individual countries
• the effectiveness of these responses.

World issue: Politics of development

Candidates may refer to:
• bilateral aid
• weaknesses in aid programmes and accusations of corruption in spending
• UK Department for International Development responses
• USAID
• NGOs from individual countries
• Chinese investment across Africa.

Any other valid point that meets the criteria described in the general marking instructions for this kind of question.

Possible approach to answering this question:

Response
The UK Department for International Development is responsible for spending a budget of £8 billion on programmes that are designed to improve infrastructure in health, education and food security. (1 mark KU) However, there are many criticisms of development aid as it can be difficult to prevent corruption within the country from redirecting the funds elsewhere.
(1 mark analysis)

Total 2 marks — 1 mark KU, 1 mark analysis.

World issue: Conflict in Syria

Candidates may refer to:
• Russian/USA/UK/French military action and support
• Saudi Arabian and Iranian intervention
• economic sanctions
• diplomatic support to negotiate peace
• humanitarian support and responses to the refugee crisis.

Any other valid point that meets the criteria described in the general marking instructions for this kind of question.

Possible approaches to answering this question:

Response 1
Countries have tried to intervene in the Syrian war through military interventions. Donald Trump recently authorised air strikes against Assad's troops in response to a chemical weapons attack on rebel held areas. (1 mark KU)

Total 1 mark — 1 mark KU.

Response 2
The USA has responded to the Syrian Civil War by imposing economic sanctions on Syrian banks in an attempt to pressurise the Assad government to stop fighting and negotiate peace. These sanctions make the transfer of funds into the country nearly impossible and could bankrupt the Syrian government. (2 marks KU) However, they have not been effective in reducing the power of the Syrian government as a black market trade in money has developed instead. (1 mark analysis) The USA has also banned US products from being exported to Syria. This has also not been effective as the Syrian government is still able to access what it needs from partners such as Iran and Russia, while the trade ban prevents aid agencies from using medical equipment made in the USA. (1 mark KU, 1 mark analysis) Overall, this shows that the economic sanctions imposed by the USA have largely failed to provide an effective response to the crisis as they have not forced Assad to negotiate peace and have only worsened the impact on those suffering in the war. (1 mark evaluation)

Total 6 marks — 3 marks KU, 2 marks analysis, 1 mark evaluation.</td></tr>
</table>

General marking principles for Higher Modern Studies Paper 2

Marking principles for each question type

For each of the question types the following provides an overview of marking principles.

The information handling questions used in this paper are
- to what extent is it accurate to state that ... **10 marks**
- what conclusions can be drawn ... **10 marks**
- to what extent are sources ... reliable **8 marks**

Objectivity questions (10 marks)

- Award up to **3 marks** for a single developed point depending on the use of the evidence in the sources and the quality of the analysis or evaluation.
- Award marks where candidates synthesise information both within and between sources.
- For **full marks** candidates must refer to all sources in their answer.
- Candidates must also make an overall judgement as to the extent of the accuracy of the given statement. Award a maximum of **8 marks** if no overall judgement is made on extent of accuracy of the statement.

Conclusions questions (10 marks)

- Award up to **3 marks** for a single developed point depending on the use of the evidence in the sources and the quality of the analysis or evaluation.
- Award marks where candidates synthesise information both within and between sources.
- For **full marks** candidates must refer to all sources in their answer.
- Candidates are required to make an overall conclusion about the issue in the question. Award a maximum of **8 marks** if candidates do not provide an overall conclusion

Reliability questions (8 marks)

- Award up to **2 marks** for a single developed point depending on the use of the evidence in the sources and the quality of the analysis and/or evaluation.
- For **full marks** candidates must refer to all sources in their answer.
- Candidates must also make a judgement based on the evidence on the most reliable source. Award a maximum of **6 marks** if candidates do not provide an overall judgement.
- Award a maximum of **3 marks** if only one factor is considered, for example, date, bias, sample size, provenance.

Higher Modern Studies marking grid for 10 mark source based (objectivity/conclusions) questions

	1 mark	2 marks	3 marks	4 marks	5 marks	6 marks	7 marks	8 marks
Use of sources of evidence. Award up to **8 marks.**	Candidate uses one relevant piece of evidence from one source relating to one aspect of the issue.	Candidate links two distinct pieces of evidence relating to one aspect of the issue which may be from within a single source or between sources.	Candidate synthesises two distinct pieces of evidence relating to one aspect of the issue which may be from within a single source or between sources, and gives an evaluative comment.	In addition, the candidate addresses a second aspect of the issue with reference to one relevant piece of evidence.	In addition, the candidate addresses a second aspect of the issue with reference to linked evidence.	In addition, the candidate addresses a second aspect of the issue is addressed with reference to synthesised evidence including an evaluative comment.	In addition, the candidate addresses a third aspect of the issue with reference to one relevant piece of evidence.	In addition, the candidate addresses a third aspect of the issue with reference to linked evidence **OR** synthesised evidence including an evaluative comment.
Objectivity Candidate presents an analysis of the accuracy/ selectivity/ objectivity of a given view against the evidence. Award up to **2 marks.**	Candidate provides an objective assessment of a given view, based on evidence presented from the sources.	Candidate provides a detailed objective assessment of a given view, based on evidence presented from the sources.	1. For **full marks** candidates **must** refer to all sources in their answer. Award a maximum of **6 marks** if all sources are not used. 2. **Objectivity questions** • Award up to **8 marks** for an accurate evaluation of the given view using evidence. • Award up to **2 marks** for an overall judgement as to the extent of accuracy and/or objectivity of the view. 3. **Conclusions questions** For **full marks** candidates **must** make evaluative comments or judgement(s) or draw a conclusion about each of the points given in the question. Award a further **2 marks** for an overall conclusion.					
Conclusion Candidate presents an overall evaluative comment(s) derived from a judgement of the evidence. Award up to **2 marks.**	Candidate presents an overall conclusion that is clear and supported by evidence from the sources.	Candidate presents an overall conclusion that is insightful and supported by detailed evidence from the sources.						

Higher Modern Studies marking grid for 8 mark source based (reliability) questions

	1 mark	2 marks	3 marks	4 marks	5 marks	6 marks
Use of sources of evidence. Award up to **6 marks.**	Candidate uses one relevant piece of evidence accurately to explain the reliability of one source.	Candidate uses one relevant piece of evidence accurately to explain in detail the reliability of one source. **OR** Candidate uses two distinct pieces of evidence accurately to explain the reliability of one source.	In addition, the candidate uses one relevant piece of evidence accurately to explain the reliability of a second source.	In addition, the candidate uses one relevant piece of evidence accurately to explain in detail the reliability of a second source. **OR** Candidate uses two distinct pieces of evidence accurately to explain the reliability of a second source.	In addition, the candidate uses one relevant piece of evidence accurately to explain the reliability of a third source.	In addition, the candidate uses one relevant piece of evidence accurately to explain in detail the reliability of a third source. **OR** Candidate uses two distinct pieces of evidence accurately to explain the reliability of a third source.
Reliability Candidate presents an overall evaluative comment(s) on which source is the most reliable, derived from a judgement of the evidence. Award up to **2 marks.**	Candidate presents an overall conclusion on the most reliable source, that is clear and supported by evidence from the sources.	Candidate presents an overall conclusion on the most reliable source, that is insightful and supported by detailed evidence from all the sources.	1. For **full marks** candidates **must** refer to all sources in their answer. Award a maximum of **5 marks** if all sources are not used. Award a maximum of **3 marks** if only one factor is considered, for example date, bias, sample size, provenance. 2. Award up to **6 marks** for an accurate evaluation of source reliability. Award a further **2 marks** for an overall judgement on the most reliable source.			

Conclusions question

Question		General Marking Instructions	Max marks	Specific Marking Instructions for this question
1.		Candidates interpret and/or evaluate complex sources in order to reach conclusions. In order to gain marks candidates must show evidence which explains the conclusions reached. • Award up to **3 marks** where candidates use evidence appropriately, depending on the quality of the explanation and the synthesis of the evidence to reach any one conclusion. • For **full marks** candidates must refer to all sources in their answer. • For **full marks** candidates must reach conclusions about each of the points given and make an overall conclusion on the issue.	10	Candidates can be credited in a number of ways **up to a maximum of 10 marks.** **Possible approaches to answering the question:** **The impact of minimum unit pricing on consumption by socio-economic group.** **Response 1** The impact of MUP has lowered consumption levels for poorer people. Source C shows that those from social classes CDE drink 2 units less than they did before MUP. **Total — 1 mark (conclusion with supporting evidence).** **Response 2** MUP has had a mixed impact on consumption by socio-economic group. Source A states that those who live in poverty now drink less. This is backed up by Source C which shows that social classes CDE have cut down their drinking but it also shows that social classes A and B have not. **Total — 2 marks (conclusion with supporting evidence synthesised from Sources A and C).** **Response 3** The impact of MUP has lowered consumption levels for poorer people but made no difference to the middle and upper classes. Source C shows that those from social classes CDE drink 2 units less than they did before MUP was introduced, whereas those from social classes AB remain unchanged, still drinking 12 units per week. This is supported by Source A where it states that 'drinkers who live in poverty used to purchase approximately 500 units of alcohol per year, for less than 50p per unit, however after a year of MUP this figure has decreased. Interestingly, this has not been the case with those in better off socio-economic groups (A and B).' **Total — 3 marks (conclusion with synthesis of evidence from Source C and then synthesised with Source A).** **The impact of minimum unit pricing on crime rates.** **Response 4** MUP has had no impact on crime rates. 60% of young offenders were drunk at the time of their offence, often having consumed strong tonic wine which is priced above 50p per unit. **Total — 1 mark (conclusion with supporting evidence from Source A).** **Response 5** High tariff crimes such as murder and violence show a small decrease in recent years but it is debateable whether this has any relation to MUP (Source A). This is shown in Source B where both violent and hate crimes have decreased since MUP was introduced but only by a small amount. Source A also states that MUP might have actually caused a crime increase as supermarkets have reported a rise in theft. Overall, MUP has had little impact on crime rates and may have actually made crime worse. **Total — 3 marks (evidence from Source A synthesised with Source B, then the use of Source A with conclusion).** **The impact of minimum unit pricing on health.** **Response 6** Source B shows that alcohol related hospital admissions are decreasing in Scotland and increasing in England. Source A states that Scotland was the first country in the world to have MUP, and England doesn't yet have it. This shows that MUP has had an impact on lowering alcohol related health issues in Scotland. **Total — 2 marks (Source B synthesised with Source A with conclusion).**

Question		General Marking Instructions	Max marks	Specific Marking Instructions for this question
1.		(continued)		**Response 7** Source A states that MUP aims to make dangerous 'binge drinking' more expensive and that 'binge drinking' is a major cause of hospitalisation. This links with Source B which shows that alcohol related hospital admissions in Scotland have reduced since MUP was introduced in 2018 and it shows that it is projected to continue to decrease. Source B also shows that alcohol related hospital admissions in England are actually rising and they do not have a MUP yet (Source A). This shows that MUP appears to be working in improving health. **Total — 3 marks (Source A synthesised with Source B, evaluative comment and conclusion).** **Possible overall conclusion on the extent to which people's drinking habits have changed due to minimum unit pricing.** **Response 8** I conclude overall that MUP has changed the drinking habits of some groups but the majority of people (63%) have continued to drink in the same way. **Total — 1 mark (overall conclusion supported by evidence from Source A).** **Response 9** I conclude overall that MUP has changed the drinking habits of some groups but not women overall whose consumption stays the same according to Source C. **Total — 1 mark (overall conclusion supported by evidence from Source C).** **Response 10** I conclude overall that MUP has changed the drinking habits of some groups but the majority of people (63%) have continued to drink in the same way. It has reduced consumption of alcohol in lower class groups but critics argue that it is not the 'prosecco drinking well-to-do in society that minimum pricing affects, it is the everyday person trying to buy a drink that he or she can afford' (Source A). This means it has not worked fully to change drinking habits. **Total — 2 marks (overall conclusion supported by detailed evidence).** *Any other valid point that meets the criteria described in the general marking principles for this type of question.* **Do not award marks for a valid conclusion which is not supported with relevant source evidence.**

Objectivity question

Question		General Marking Instructions	Max marks	Specific Marking Instructions for this question
2.		Candidates interpret and/ or evaluate complex sources of information, detecting and explaining the extent of objectivity. In order to gain marks candidates must show evidence which supports the extent of accuracy in a given viewpoint. • Award up to **3 marks** where candidates use evidence appropriately, depending on the quality of the explanation and the synthesis of the evidence, for any one explanation of the extent of objectivity. • For **full marks** candidates must refer to all sources in their answer. • For **full marks** candidates must make an overall judgement as to the extent of the accuracy of the given statement.	10	Candidates can gain marks in a number of ways up to a maximum of 10 marks. **Evidence that supports the view: 'that efforts to reduce the threat posed by nuclear weapons have been successful'.** **Examples of types of evidence that support the view include:** • New START Treaty targets met by both Russia and the USA (Source B) • 'the advantages and successes of the New START deal so far will improve the likelihood of a renewal of the Treaty' (Source B) • treaty on the Prohibition on Nuclear Weapons agreed to by 122 countries (Source A) • treaty on the Prohibition of Nuclear Weapons signed by UN Secretary General and 'celebrated as a step towards a nuclear free world.' (Source A) • public opinion poll – 57% agree that there is a reduced threat from nuclear weapons (Source A) • four out of the five nuclear weapon states have reduced their stockpiles from 1985 levels (Source B) • the number of global nuclear warheads has fallen by over 50,000 between 1985 and 2017. (Source B) **Possible approaches to answering the question:** **Response 1** The statement is supported by evidence because Source B shows that four out of five nuclear weapons states have all reduced their total global nuclear warheads stockpile since 1985. **Total – 1 mark (evidence used from one source).** **Response 2** The statement is supported by evidence because there has been a reduction in the number of nuclear weapons. Source A shows that in 2010 the New START Treaty between the USA and Russia set a target of reducing their strategic warheads by February 2018. Source B shows that both Russia and the USA achieved this target, Russia with a massive reduction of over 30,000 since 1985. Source B also shows that the *'advantages and successes of the New START deal so far will improve the likelihood of a renewal of the Treaty'* in 2021 showing that the process of nuclear disarmament should continue. **Total – 3 marks (synthesis of evidence from Sources A and B with evaluative comment).** **Evidence that opposes the view: 'that efforts to reduce the threat posed by nuclear weapons have been successful'.** **Examples of types of evidence that oppose the view include:** • increase in number of states with nuclear warheads since 1965 (Source B) • nuclear weapon states have refused to attend the treaty negotiations (Source A) • heightened tensions as a result of tweets by Donald Trump (Source B) • North Korea 'has now conducted six nuclear tests' (Source B) • withdrawal of the USA from Iran deal (Source B) • uncertainty over New START renewal (Source B).

Question		General Marking Instructions	Max marks	Specific Marking Instructions for this question
2.		(continued)		**Response 3** The statement is inaccurate because Source B shows that there is growing tension between America and North Korea over the North's development of nuclear weapons. North Korea now has 15 warheads in their stockpile and Donald Trump has threatened to *'totally destroy'* North Korea and said that he too has a *'nuclear button, but it is much bigger and more powerful one'* than North Korea's which is true as the USA still has 4000 nuclear warheads. This shows that one of the main nuclear weapons states continues to threaten to use nuclear weapons showing that efforts to reduce the threat have not been successful. **Total — 3 marks (synthesis of evidence within one source with evaluative comment).** For **full marks,** candidates **must** make an overall judgement as to the extent of the accuracy of the given statement. **Examples of possible overall judgements:** • the statement that efforts to reduce the threat posed by nuclear weapons have been successful is accurate **(0 marks)** • overall it is not accurate to state that efforts to reduce the threat of nuclear weapons have been successful **(0 marks)** • overall it is largely accurate to state that efforts to reduce the threat of nuclear weapons have been successful. Whilst there has been an increase in the number of states with nuclear weapons, the number of weapons that they have is relatively small in comparison to the amount that Russia and the USA have. The success of the New START Treaty has led to a significant reduction in the overall number of warheads Russia and USA have and shows that there is now a much smaller threat posed by nuclear weapons than in the past **(2 marks)** • overall it is only true to a very small extent to say that the efforts to reduce the threat have been successful because the President of the USA has clearly been threatening other countries with use of nuclear weapons and so whilst they have fewer warheads than in the past, the threat remains a significant one as only one missile could create significant destruction **(2 marks)** • the statement is partially true as while the number of warheads has decreased, enough remain in the world for the threat to still exist. **(1 mark)**

Reliability question

Question		General Marking Instructions	Max marks	Specific Marking Instructions for this question
3.		Candidates interpret and/or evaluate three complex sources of information, evaluating and explaining the extent or reliability. In order to gain marks candidates must show evidence which supports the evaluations reached. • Award up to **2 marks** where candidates use evidence appropriately, depending on the quality of the explanation and the synthesis of the evidence, for any one explanation of the extent of reliability. • For **full marks** candidates must refer to all sources in their answer. • For **full marks** candidates must make an overall conclusion on the most reliable source of information.	8	Candidates can gain marks in a number of ways up to a maximum of **8 marks.** **Source A** **Response 1** Source A is reliable. **Total — 0 marks (no evidence or explanation provided).** **Response 2** Source A can be seen as not reliable as it is out of date. The opinion of the public may have changed since then. **Total — 1 mark (straightforward evidence provided).** **Response 3** Source A is mostly reliable and trustworthy. It comes from a respected polling company (Ipsos Mori) with a reputation to protect and in its research it asked a large sample of over 1000 voters. This should help ensure that the information presented is representative. **Total — 2 marks (detailed evidence provided).**

Question		General Marking Instructions	Max marks	Specific Marking Instructions for this question
3.		(continued)		**Source B** **Response 4** Source B can be viewed as not being reliable as it comes from a political campaign group (Vote Leave) and could be biased. **Total — 1 mark (straightforward evidence provided).** **Response 5** Source B can be viewed as not being reliable as it comes from a political campaign group (Vote Leave) and could be biased. It also gives a figure (£350m per week) but hasn't included any evidence or a reference as to where the information came from. This makes it difficult to check this figure and therefore calls into question how reliable this source is. **Total — 2 marks (detailed evidence provided).** **Source C** **Response 6** Source C can be viewed as not being reliable as it is produced by a political party and therefore could be considered biased. **Total — 1 mark (straightforward evidence provided).** **Response 7** Source C can be viewed as not being reliable as the presentation of the graph indicates that the information has been manipulated as the differences in the figures and the bar graphs are not proportionate and give the impression that the gap between the Green Party and the Conservatives is larger than it actually is. **Total — 2 marks (detailed evidence provided).** **Examples of an overall conclusion on the most reliable source of information:** **Response 8** Source A is the most reliable source as it comes from a reputable source and contains a very high number of respondents to the survey. **Total — 1 mark (overall conclusion supported by evidence from one source).** **Response 9** Source A is the most reliable source as it comes from a reputable source and contains a very high number of respondents to the survey. The information may be out of date, however, when compared to the other two sources which come from potentially biased organisations such as political parties and campaign groups, it is the most reliable of the three. **Total 2 marks (overall conclusion supported by detailed evidence from all sources).** For **full marks,** candidates **must** make an overall judgement on the most reliable source.

Acknowledgements

Permission has been sought from all relevant copyright holders and Hodder Gibson is grateful for the use of the following:

Source A: Article is adapted from '"Jihadi Jack" Letts interview: Former Oxford schoolboy calls on British people to convert to Islam as he brands David Cameron an "evil creature"' by Shebab Khan, taken from The Independent, 30 January 2016 (2018 SQP page 7);
Source B: Graph is adapted from 'Issues facing Britain – What do you see as the biggest issue facing the UK today?' © Ipsos MORI (2018 SQP page 7);
Source C: Screenshot of Channel 4 News website – "Do we know why we're in Afghanistan" by Jon Snow, 28 July 2009 © Channel 4 TV (2018 SQP page 8);
Source A: © Ipsos Mori 2011 (https://www.ipsos.com/sites/default/files/migrations/en-uk/files/Assets/Docs/Scotland/scottish-public-opinion-monitor-decmber-2011-tables-part-2.pdf (2019 page 8);
Source B: Image © Christopher Furlong/gettyimages.com (2019 page 8);
Source C: A leaflet reproduced by permission of The Green Party (2019 page 9).